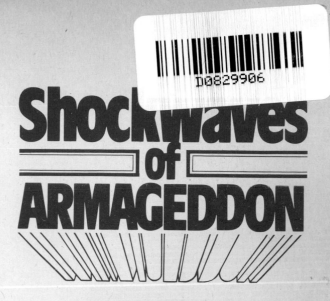

Shockwaves of ARMAGEDDON

DOUG CLARK

HARVEST HOUSE PUBLISHERS
Eugene, Oregon 97402

SHOCKWAVES OF ARMAGEDDON

DEDICATION

This exposé on Biblical prophecy and current events exploding all around us today is dedicated to the thousands of viewers of our television program "Shockwaves of Armageddon," seen coast-to-coast on the Trinity Broadcasting Network.

Our program is heard four times weekly from California to Florida on the major stations of TBN, and throughout the nation on cable.

To you, the viewers, with your keen interest in Biblical prophecy, I dedicate this book, answering the questions you are asking daily in the mail and on the phone.

FOREWORD

Week after week the wires of the Associated Press and related news media convey messages of shocking events that seem to fit the scenarios of prophecy presented by John in the Book of Revelation and by Daniel in his marvelous predictions of the Old Testament.

The return of the Jew to the land, the rise of the Magog (Soviet) nation, the emergence of the Orientals to the world scene, the problem of Arab oil states and Israel, the unique merger of ten nations together out of the old Roman Empire—and much, much more—all lead us to believe that we are the end-time generation that Jesus spoke of in Luke 21:32: "This generation shall not pass away till all be fulfilled."

No one knows the day or the hour when the Son of Man will return to judge the world, but we do know that things are catapulting in on us fast. Prophesied events of hundreds and hundreds of years ago are now coming to pass.

The events of today are rapidly pushing us into the millennial state which we all so much anticipate and long for. Soon the "night season" will be over and the day will dawn. But until then the night is getting darker as the hours deepen.

We currently walk the razor's edge of the most profound prophecies in history. The human race is on a crash course with God. This collision of man with divine justice will be cataclysmic and soon.

—Doug Clark

CONTENTS

Foreword

1

Shockwaves from the United States

She rose to the greatest position of power, prestige, and glory of any nation in world history. She stormed the world with her productivity, affected the world with her freedoms for all, and impressed everyone with her gospel fervor and zeal for truth.

This was and is America the Great. She ranks ahead of the nations mentioned in the Bible, such as Magog-Russia, Egypt, Persia, Libya, Ethiopia, Africa, Asia, and Europe. Even Rome and Athens in all their glory could never begin to compare with the might and power of America.

Of all the shocking subjects of Biblical prophecy, such as the coming world dictator, the Antichrist, the False Prophet, the Great Tribulation Period, The mark of the Beast credit card, and the Battle of Armageddon, only the majesty of the doctrine of the second coming of Christ exceeds in interest how America fits into the Biblical panorama of events foretold in the Word of God.

America is not mentioned by name in the Bible, but she is certainly alluded to in Ezekiel 38:13, when she is mentioned as a young lion of Tarshish, questioning Russia's advance on the nation of Israel in the prophesied war of the red horse of Revelation 6.

History reveals that Tarshish was and is Spain. Spain in her earlier days was a mighty force to be reckoned with (in Biblical days). She had come to America and Canada long before Columbus. Archeological finds tell us that the Spaniards were the first to come here.

Ezekiel had a vision of this, and he stated that the offspring of Tarshish—the young lions—would be alive and well when Moscow invaded Jerusalem at the end time.

It was no mistake that America was born, for without her powers given by God, many prophecies would not be fulfilled yet, nor would others be fulfilled without her. God ordained the United States of America and endued her with the most unique powers of any nation on earth to fulfill the task He had and has for her.

God planned for America to be the end-time nation so strong as to ensure that the Biblical prophecies would be carried out by this human instrument of the Lord.

No nation has ever succeeded in offering the world more than America has in her smorgasbord of nationalities, who came here for the greatest opportunities known to the human race.

If we ever see the death of the American dream, this country will still always be remembered as the nation of the two-car family and the four-bedroom house with the lovely pool out back and the landscaped lawn out front.

America is known the world over as the land of plenty. She produces the world's greatest amounts of foods, fruits, and meats, and she exports the most of any nation (more than most nations joined together), while at the same time enabling her own people to have the richest diet in the world.

America is free enterprise. You can immigrate here to America on a shoestring and become a millionaire if you have the enterprising spirit and know-how with which to do so.

There are more millionaires in America than in all the rest of the world put together.

We run 75 percent of the world's cars, trucks, airplanes, computers, and television and radio stations. We have the world's finest hospitals, science, and superhighways, as well as the best and most of the world's finest inventive genius and products in virtually every home.

Though not specifically mentioned in the Biblical prophecies, America was born of God, Who knew He would use her expertise for His own ultimate glory as well as for the good of the world.

America would help mold the world into readiness for God's Son, Jesus Christ, to return the second time.

The pressures of taxes, religious persecution, industrial weaknesses, and hardships of life in England and Europe drove their people to migrate to the new land. They came by the thousands from Ireland to Italy, from Norway to Greece, to make this country the home of the brave and the land of the free.

They braved new hardships, carved out a nation, drove out would-be invaders, and formed a Constitution, a Bill of Rights, and a government for the people, by the people, and of the people that was an astonishment to the world.

God knew that what was happening was in His will for this nation. He wanted a strong free-enterprise system, flourishing for the benefit of the world and the fulfillment of His Word.

God saw to it that the nation was not divided into two countries in the Civil War—something envisioned by the Europeans, who helped plan this divisive war for their own gains.

Equal rights for all men was the key to the country's greatness, in spite of prejudice that is still here, though shrinking today.

Freedom to write, speak, preach, teach, engage in legitimate business, prosper, and create its own monetary system was part of the reward for the hard work of the people who made this nation possible.

The free democracy that developed through the halls of Congress and their ensuing important documents that would be the guidelines for the years to come for the people was all part of God's plan to help fulfill the amazing Biblical prophecies.

From the founding of this nation, God has had a hand in all the steps that led this nation to its greatness.

Because America was founded on freedom from government restraint in business—freedom from government intervention in the free-enterprise system—and because of the free spirit of man, this nation became the birthplace of modern science and its worldwide blessings.

For 5000 years the world was in the grips of "wood, water, and the wheel." Then came the Americans with their science of electricity and the world-revolutionizing development of scientific discoveries that baffle the modern mind right up until today.

Americans were the first in computer sciences, oil-drilling equipment, auto and truck-building expertise, airplanes and supersonic aerial equipment, and the marvels of communication and telecommunications, to say nothing of splitting the atom and developing nuclear fission, thus plunging the world into the age of science as the development and discovery of oil as energy and black gold came into being simultaneously.

Now picture America in the early 40's. She was recovering beautifully from the 1929 great depression. The free-enterprise system was really working. There was almost no inflation. Dollar creation and credit for the government was limited to the amount of gold on hand in Fort Knox. The nation had not yet demonetized its gold storage.

War was on in Europe, with Germany and Hitler attempting to conquer the world on many fronts.

England was weakening, and France, Holland, Belgium, Poland, and other nations had fallen to Germany.

Russia was fighting against Germany, but was losing too.

Then America declared war and plunged in with American spirit, expertise, money, manpower and a military effectiveness that drove the Germans out of North Africa, and Rommel with them. Americans drove them back as they plunged into Europe, and with Allied help from Australia, Canada, and West Europe, as well as the mighty patriotic underground of the occupied nations, the U.S. drove the Nazis back to Berlin to the end of Hitler and his gang.

What had America accomplished?

The freedom of the nations of Europe from fascism. From Norway to Greece, from Ireland to Italy, the Europeans were free from tyranny, although Eastern Europe was falling into a Soviet camp.

The Russians divided Germany and Berlin. It was no doubt part of God's plan to punish the Germans for their treatment of the Jews.

Russia had already extended her Communist control over Estonia, Latvia, and Lithuania and was moving against Poland, Czechoslovakia, Hungary, etc.

Europe was being divided again. It was the eventual Warsaw Pact forces of the Communists against the Americans, Europeans, and Canadians in the NATO forces (North Atlantic Treaty Organization).

Russia thanked the West for helping her out of German annihilation by taking over every nation she could.

But did not Ezekiel 38:1-6 state that Magog (Russia) would advance in a great war against Israel with Gomer and Togarmah, grandsons of Noah, who became nations in Eastern Europe? Yes, Ezekiel predicted this more than 2700 years ago.

From 1930 until now the Soviets (as the Russians prefer to be called) have expanded in keeping with Bible prophecy, and now are expanding into the Middle East as also predicted in that passage, now that they are in Afghanistan and are working with Iraq, Iran, Syria, the PLO, Libya, and Ethiopia— exactly as the prophet stated under divine inspiration.

But the United States was raised up by God to help stop fascism and halt the spread of Communism in Europe, thus making possible the amazing prophecies of the Bible, including those stated repeatedly in Daniel and Revelation—that ten nations would rise out of the old Roman Empire and form a government for the Antichrist to take over ultimately.

America kept free those nations of Western Europe by her strength so that these important prophecies could be fulfilled (Daniel 2, Daniel 7, and Revelation 17:12). We will go into detail on these verses later, but suffice it to say now that, without America, where would Europe be, and the fulfillment of these propheices?

God knew what He was doing, and He always does.

America was raised up to fulfill the prophecies of the Bible, as sure as you understand the prophecies being fulfilled today.

We held the enemy back when it was right and proper and in the will of God for us to hold them back.

We let them advance and even helped build their empires with our scientific expertise when it was not to our national advantage to do so, but it was obviously the will of God for us to do so.

Multinational banks of America and Europe kept the Soviet system financially afloat when it was doomed to failure during the past 50 years.

Wall Street bankers and leaders in New York and London have financed the Bolshevik Revolution and expansion of the industries of the Soviet Union to the tune of billions of American dollars!

It is unbelievable, but we have helped them with low-interest loans, outright gifts of money, and our best science. They have built to our specifications factories, oil wells, and oil rigs. We have sold them our food and taught them our scientific secrets, knowing that we would fight them someday!

Please see my books entitled *How to Survive the*

Money Crash and *The Coming Oil War.* Notes are in the back as to how to get good books on economics, war, and the future economically and politically for America.

I will not rewrite that material here, but you should know that we built the Soviet Union to a large extent with American dollars and companies because we are hungry for profit from the Communists. We totally disregard the well-being of Americans in the future because of our interest in making money right now.

Now we are starting to build China with the same techniques we used in Russia, helping them with oil, machinery, plastics, chemicals, food, industry, etc. Recently we sold them military planes, etc., thereby readying China for the Battle of Armageddon.

God is using and has used America and her brains not only to protect Europe from her enemies, but also to lead us into the Biblically predicted coming oil war and the one-world government.

There are political organizations and multinational business corporations in the U.S. and Canada promoting as hard as they can the theme of one-world government.

They want the power, the unbelievable wealth and the control over nations and humans, that will come through this channel. *And they will get it!* Events that fulfill prophecy cannot change, nor should we want them to change, since they will hasten the return of the Lord Jesus Christ to His throne in Jerusalem, bringing peace and justice for all the deprived of this world, and an end to all wars and bloodshed.

The very system of commerce that made this nation so great, the free-enterprise system, is under attack. The only basic lesson in economics that I would like to give in this book is that when you inflate the money supply of any nation you have inflation. By this I mean that in the U.S. there is the Federal Reserve System determining the money supply for credit money to be placed into the banking system, as well as cash on a daily basis.

When the Fed inflates the amount of credit available to the banks and the government, and increases the supply of money dramatically, this creates too much money simultaneously with high interest rates.

This is inflation of the money supply. But the money does not go to general businesses of the nation to help promote growth in the country and economic well-being in the free-enterprise system. Instead, it is all dammed up with a wall of high interest, and thus it becomes an ocean of money on the other side of the dam.

If the money is being created by the system as legislated by Congress for them to do so, but the money is not reaching the businessman because he cannot afford the exorbitant interest rates to secure it, then where is it going?

It is currently paying for government budgets,

which are at an all-time high—to the tune of billions of dollars more than last year!

International bankers, who control the creation of money in each country, love high government budgets of those respective countries, because this means they can loan billions to the governments, charge them high interest (which they get by taking government bonds for the bills they exchange), and thus become rich as the governments go further into debt.

Big government budgets please the central bankers of any country. Central Bankers (of the Fed) also control the interest rates, and can set them high or low.

Low interest rates mean that the money created flows to the general business marketplace of the nation, creating jobs and products, and thereby demand for more products and personnel. This greatly increases the Gross National Product (GNP) of the nation. Low interest rates mean that business prospers, the free-enterprise system succeeds, and the nation grows to new economic heights.

High interest rates cut business production, increase unemployment, increase welfare recipients, decrease production of goods and services, induce an economic breakdown of the free-enterprise system which is unwittingly sanctioned by government actions. Usually these government actions are done by men who do not understand economics.

The legislators are told that this is the way to

save the country from inflation or depression. But instead it always produces depression and inflation, thereby killing the dream of that country. This has always been true in history and is widely repeating itself today. We fail to learn from the past and are being deceived by "evil men waxing worse and worse and being deceived" (2 Timothy 3:13).

The plan is to destroy the currency through inflation and high interest rates; corrupt the judicial system and make it easier for crime to flourish through weakened laws; stifle initiative in business; create bankruptcies for the stubborn who resist; poison the minds of youth and others with drugs and filth on the screen at home and the local theaters; precipitate an oil war that will put the nation in shambles; then maneuver the enemy into a powerful position militarily, while simultaneously managing an oil embargo or cutoff over Israel's intransigence regarding the new Palestinian demands.

With oil cut off in retaliation from the Moslem world against Americans (for not pressuring Israel into giving up Jerusalem and the West Bank for the Palestinians), we are lost without adequate supplies of energy for every need in the country.

Business will fail; the stock market will collapse; the government will go bankrupt. The nation will go hungry, with jobless millions ready for any kind of an answer, especially if they have to go to war at this time of energy shortages. That will only compound the matter, for the government will use almost all the available oil for military purposes.

Is this the plan of God? If you believe that the powers that be are ordained of God (Romans 13:1), and if you believe that prophecy must be fulfilled in order to bring about the return of Christ, then this must be of God. Naturally, this leaves us with somewhat mixed emotions if we are both patriotic and Christian.

But patriotism must never take the place of God's highest plan and will for men. We are not citizens of this world (Ephesians 2:19) if we have been transformed by the regenerating power of Christ in salvation. We are citizens of heaven, from whence we look for the coming of the Lord.

America was raised up to do the job of protecting when God wanted her to protect, as in the case of Europe and the protection from the Nazis.

She was raised up economically and industrially stronger than any other nation in order to make other nations strong when that was God's will, even if those nations were the ones that she was destined to fight, and would face her own skills and scientific expertise in the battlefields of the world.

Now God has apparently allowed Satan to raise up in America those insidiously moving forces that are engulfing this nation and are promoting unprecedented failure through economic tragedies such as inflation, high interest rates, and a general undermining of the free-enterprise system and the general morals of the nation.

But as we look at the whole world objectively and realize that the greatest event, the most blessed epoch that could change this world completely, would be the coming of the Lord Jesus Christ, then it is easier to accept what is happening.

When we pray faithfully "Thy kingdom come," we may find ourselves actually praying for the demise of our land unconsciously and unwittingly.

Would it be possible that in order for His kingdom to come America might have to go through some terrible days?

Yes, that is possible.

America deserves a judging from God, as do all nations. America has not been perfect, nor have we professed to be.

We cannot correct the wrongs and injustices and disorders and blemishes of the past. They are done, and we are living now. God will bring punitive damages to the nation for all those misdeeds.

As Christians we need to pray about the impending evils that this nation threatens to get herself involved with.

1. Tolerance of our nation toward homosexuality is a terrible evil. God never meant for a nation to allow itself to nationally recognize and promote such evil. Nations that have done this in the past have all disappeared into the dust of the ages as far as world power is concerned.

2. Arming Israel's enemies is against God's will.

This is enough to frighten the best of us when we consider that every nation that ever came against Israel in the past either does not exist today or is a third-world nation with no productivity and begs from others for a living while enduring the worst of living standards for her people.

God loves the homosexual and God loves Israel's enemies (He has salvation for all of them through Jesus Christ), but ours is not to aid their cause, but rather to pray for them, work kindly with them, and show them a more excellent way.

2

Shockwaves from Israel

No nation of people has commanded more world attention nor surrounded themselves with more intrigue than Israel of yesterday and today.

In the Old Testament it was repeatedly prophesied that they would go into bondage and captivity if they continued to disobey God in failing to worship Him alone and to keep His Sabbath year free from labor.

But they failed Him, and He allowed the captivity to take place for over 70 years, as prophesied (Jeremiah 29:10; Daniel 9:24-27).

The Jews were constantly under the yoke of conquerors, and then were made free, only to become enslaved again after disobeying God and His plan for them.

The Egyptians and Assyrians conquered them. The Babylonians conquered them. Then came the Medes and Persians, and following them was Alexander the Great with the Greco-Macedonians.

Then came Rome, and since then many conquerors have entered the Holy Land, and the Jews have been dispersed to the four corners of the earth.

Their first temple was destroyed under Nebuchadnezzar and the Babylonians, and then came captivity for them.

They came home to build again under Nehemiah, Ezra, Zechariah, and Haggai. Jerusalem took shape and so did the temple. It was destroyed as Jesus predicted in A.D. 70 under the murdering Romans, under whose jurisdiction Jesus was crucified, as the Jews rejected Him as their Messiah and Savior.

They looked for a Messiah who would be a King and deliver them from bondage. But instead He came as the son of a carpenter, and He went to the cross for their sins.

They could not see the lowly Nazarene fulfilling their anticipations. They failed to see and listen to Isaiah 53, about the suffering Servant atoning for their sins. They could not see or hear the Prophet Daniel in chapter 9:26 describing the Messiah being cut off, but not for Himself.

They could not understand about this suffering Messiah or His role as the sacrificial Lamb, to atone for the sins of Israel and the world.

They rejected Him: "He came to His own, and His own received Him not" (John 1:11).

God let them wander in a spiritual wilderness, even as they wandered with Moses for 38 unnecessary years after Sinai. But he promised He would bring them back again to salvation and to the land that He swore to Abraham was theirs forever (Genesis 12:1-3).

But in order to come back to God spiritually they would have to be gathered from out of the nations of the world, and led and even forced to come home and carve out a nationhood for themselves. No one else would do it for them.

Hitler was allowed to rise. The Holocaust was real. Millions of Jews died, and this act alone forced them to take the land as a result of the forced decision of the United Nations to let them go home and partition the land.

The Arabs would have nothing to do with the decision, so every foot was taken with and by the blood of these Jews wanting a homeland.

They are still dying for the homeland. The PLO makes sure they die steadily in terroristic, cowardly attacks on Israeli children and helpless civilians.

MAJOR PROPHECIES ABOUT THE JEWS

1. Jews will be dispersed to the far corners of the earth for a long period of time.

> *They shall fall by the edge of the sword, and shall be led away captive into all nations. And Jerusalem shall be trodden down of the Gentiles until the times of the Gentiles be fulfilled.*

These are the words of Jesus in Luke 21:24.

Jews have gone to the uttermost parts of the earth during this past 1900-year period.

Every nation in the industrial world (and many nations not industrialized, as in Moslem and African states) housed Jews in their ghettos.

2. Jews will be brought back to the land through bitterness.

> *I will take you from among the heathen, and gather you out of all countries, and will bring you into your own land* (Ezekiel 36:24).

They were brought back out of desperation from the conditions imposed on them in Europe. They came rich and poor, mostly the latter. They came from every country on earth to make a new world and a new country, and to have their land and nation and constitution and government. They succeeded through much pain and bloodshed to remain there until today (Ezekiel 37:11-13).

3. Israel will be attacked by the enemy from the north, and her neighbors will join this enemy.

> *After many days thou shalt be visited; in the latter years thou shalt come into the land that is brought back from the sword, and is gathered out of many people, against the mountains of Israel, which have been always waste; but it is brought forth out of the nations, and they shall dwell safely all of them* (Ezekiel 38:8).

> *In that day when my people of Israel dwelleth*
> *safely, shalt thou not know it? And thou shalt*
> *come from thy place out of the north parts—*
> *thou, and many people with thee, all of them*
> *riding upon horses, a great company, and a*
> *mighty army; and thou shalt come up against*
> *my people of Israel as a cloud to cover the*
> *land; it shall be in the latter days* (Ezekiel
> 38:14-16).

God is speaking of Magog—the Soviet Union —who will attack Israel as predicted in the "latter days," with many nations joining the Soviets against Israel. Obviously these nations are primarily the Moslems and Arab nations, who have hated Israel for coming back and coming home. They want the land for themselves, including the city of Jerusalem.

The Soviet Union is being drawn into the Moslem conflict with Israel. The Soviets want Arabian oil. They have been promised the lion's share of the oil for helping the ailing Moslem nations to defeat tiny Israel and her mainstay, the United States. The Soviets are planning this now.

The land of Magog is to rise up against Israel (Ezekiel 38:2). Magog is the grandson of Noah, who was born to Japheth, who inhabited the areas of the Gentiles as indicated in Genesis chapter 10. Magog and Tubal (his brother), plus Meshech and Togarmah, all became great regions or cities in their day and in the following centuries of time.

Magog became Russia.

Tubal became Tubolsk, the eastern capital of Russia.

Togarmah became the Turkish area of today.

Meshech became Moscow.

Gomer became the Eastern European area of Poland, Czechoslovakia, Germany, Hungary, etc.

The Soviet Union of today has taken over these areas. They are ready for the battle on two fronts:

1. The European theater of war
2. The Middle East military explosion in Israel.

Further elaborations on this will be covered later as we go into depth about what the Soviets are doing to fulfill their prophecies, even though they don't know it!

Here we are concerned primarily with Israel.

4. Israel will survive this war from the Soviets and Moslems.

Behold, I am against thee, O Gog, the chief prince of Meshech and Tubal; and I will turn thee back, and leave but the sixth part of thee, and will cause to come up from the north parts, and will bring thee upon the mountains of Israel. And I will smite thy bow out of thy left hand, and will cause thine arrows to fall out of thy right hand. Thou shalt

> *fall upon the mountains of Israel, thou, and
> all thy bands, and the people that is with
> thee. I will give thee unto the ravenous birds
> of every sort, and to the beasts of the field, to
> be devoured. Thou shalt fall upon the open
> field, for I have spoken it, saith the Lord. And
> I will send a fire on Magog, and among them
> that dwell carelessly in the isles; and they
> shall know that I am the Lord* (Ezekiel
> 39:1-6).

Here you have the nuclear disarmament of the
Soviet Union and the Warsaw Pact Forces, plus the
complete annihilation of Arab and Moslem armies
coming against Israel in this coming oil war, also
called World War Three.

It will take seven months to bury the huge
number of Arabs, Europeans, and Soviets killed in
this war (Ezekiel 39:12).

5. The timing of this war could be before Daniel's seventieth prophetic week is fulfilled.

Daniel 9:24-27 states that the Antichrist will sign
a deal with Israel to protect her for seven years. He
will then break that promise 3½ years into it, will
march on Jerusalem and Israel, and will take over
the land (Daniel 11:41,42).

One of the major reasons we are assuming that
this war is before the seven-year covenant to protect Israel is that the war could provoke the Antichrist into making this deal with Israel for
reasons that would obviously benefit him.

Note that the Scripture says:

> And they that dwell in the cities of Israel shall go forth, and shall set on fire and burn the weapons, both the shields and the bucklers, the bows and the arrows, and the handstaves and the spears, and they shall burn them with fire seven years (Ezekiel 39:9).

If Christ returns on time in His second appearance—at the end of the Tribulation Period of approximately seven years—then one could not conceive of the Israelis burning these weapons on into the millennial reign of Christ.

The Antichrist will no doubt be in power in Europe (Revelation 17:12) before the war with Russia and after various nations (such as the United States) attempt to create a buffer zone between the Arabs and the Israelis. (They are talking about creating this now if the Palestinans receive autonomy for the West Bank of the Jordan, currently being held by the Israelis.)

This treaty to protect Israel from her enemies could very well create the climate spoken of in the prophecy in which Israel is at peace, with no wall and no gates (Ezekiel 38:11,12).

Russia will then come with her Arab states and Warsaw Pact Forces, as predicted by the names of Gomer and Togarmah (Ezekiel 38:5,6) as well as Persia, Ethiopia, and Libya. (Persia of the days of the prophecy of Ezekiel covers the whole area of the Middle East from Pakistan to Turkey.)

If our timing is right concerning this great oil war, then the Antichrist would have taken over the ten nations of the prophecies of Daniel 2 and 7 and would be in the throes of tying them together, producing a new monetary unity, enlarging their nuclear capability, and making the "iron and clay" nations (as described in the prophecy) work together. (Some of them are strong—iron; some are weak—clay. Thus they need a leader. We will discuss this further in a later chapter.)

There could well be a time when the Man of Sin is first invited (Revelation 17:12) to take over the ten nations, and then actually does so. Time could and will certainly elapse as he confronts them with his program for their vital unification and enlargement.

Time will pass as he organizes them into the one-world government plan that he has.

Russia will attack on the European and Middle East fronts while the Antichrist is in power, according to Daniel 11:40. Most of this chapter (in the latter part especially) is a direct reference to the Antichrist.

The King of the North (Russia) will attack the Antichrist first, as he is the protector of the nations of Europe and is their elected leader. He represents the NATO Forces and thus represents American and Canadian interests in Europe. The U.S. presently has over 330,000 troops in Europe, with a very large financial and military commitment steadily legislated by Congress to keep Europe free from Communism.

If by that time the U.S. is still undergoing economic ills, with a depression on her hands or economic situations leading to a depression, the Antichrist will take the initiative rather than the President of the United States or any other world leader.

6. Israel has the beginnings of a mighty revival. They accept Jesus Christ as the Messiah in part.

This phenomenal spiritual awakening comes as a direct result of God's divine intervention in winning the war with the Soviets and Arabs for Israel. God said:

> *Thus will I magnify myself and sanctify myself, and I will be known in the eyes of many nations, and they shall know that I am the Lord* (Ezekiel 38:23).

There are several similar references to God magnifying Himself and revealing Himself to unbelieving Israel.

There are Jews in Israel today who believe in Jesus Christ as their Savior and Messiah. But they are not in the majority by any means. They are a tiny, very quiet minority.

Shortly after this war over oil rights and warm-water ports and the extermination of Israel, the nation will have a startling baptism of faith from the Lord.

In Romans chapters 9-11 the Apostle Paul predicted that this would happen. He spoke of the falling away of the natural branches out of God's olive tree. He spoke of the wild olive branches (the Gentiles) being grafted in.

He mentioned more than once that if the falling away of the Jews brought salvation to the Gentiles, how much more blessing would come to the world upon the return of the Jews to God.

The natural branches will be grafted back in again. This is a reference to spiritual awakenings in the hearts of the people of the Holy Land (Romans 11:11-26).

The coming oil war will startle them into recognizing the Lord of Hosts, who delivered their forefathers.

No doubt there will be a special visitation of the Holy Spirit to the people and the land, awakening dead hearts and opening blinded eyes.

Two witnesses will work miracles at proclaiming the truth and helping to bring Israel to Christ and salvation.

Zechariah chapter 4 and Revelation chapter 11 both speak of these "two witnesses" or "two candlesticks" that will stand up for the Lord rather miraculously at this time.

For 42 months, or the same period as the power of the Antichrist is enacted (and apparently at the same time of his wicked rule), these two men who are anointed of God and indestructible will preach the gospel, interrupt the program of the Antichrist, and proclaim God's power and will to the nation of Israel.

Their power could reach further than Israel, to other nations, at this time as well.

The Antichrist will attempt to have them murdered, but all attempts will fail. They will be immortal till God is through with them.

They will preach during the last 3½ years of the Tribulation with great glory and marvelous manifestations of God's power. Part of their ministry could be to other nations, reminding them of God's punishment for rejecting Christ and persecuting the Jews.

Enoch and Elijah were the only two Old Testament men taken alive to heaven by the Lord. Perhaps they will be the challengers prepared for this illustrious position. In any case, this will be one of the most exciting and interesting of all the periods of the Antichrist.

Eventually the two witnesses will be killed and translated to heaven.

The Third World War that we speak of here will be the fulfillment of the sixth chapter of Revelation, where John speaks of the apocalyptic horses riding and taking peace and food from the earth:

> *And there went out another horse that was red; and power was given to him that sat thereon to take peace from the earth, and they should kill one another; and there was given unto him a great sword* (Revelation 6:4).

This is the coming oil war. You might also note that when the Soviets (Magog) enter the Holy Land in Ezekiel 38:12, they "come to take a spoil."

Leave off the first two letters of the word *spoil* and you have the real reason the Soviets get embroiled in this war in the first place. They need energy badly, since their oil is inaccessible presently, and it is easier to help the Moslems win their war against Israel and to get the promise of oil and a warm-water port off Haifa.

Revelation 6:6 says, "See that thou hurt not the oil and the wine." Perhaps this is a reference to olive oil and grapes, food shortages and worldwide famine at this time. But there is also merit in understanding the oil as the Mideast petroleum that fuels the world.

Right after the war and famine of Revelation 6 comes the spiritual awakening of the nation of Israel in chapter 7.

A total of 144,000 Israelis will be sealed of God spiritually to be the workers of His will in Israel and perhaps other places in the world.

This is the beginning of the end of Jewish rejection of Christ as Savior and Messiah.

These Jews get an experience with Jesus Christ as their Regenerator and Justifier in the "born again" experience.

The Knesset in Israel argued vehemently among themselves as to whether they should now teach in the schools of Israel the New Testament history of the Jews, as it truly was a period of "ancient history" for them, whether they liked the teachings of Christ and His disciples or not.

The politicians were against the rabbis, who also are represented in this Israeli Parliament.

The rabbis opposed the teaching, but the politicans won the battle!

Since then thousands of Israeli children have been and are being taught the Gospels, containing the life and teachings of Jesus Christ and His truth.

They are learning of the disciples, the apostles, and the teachings of the Book of Revelation.

This seed is planted and watered by the Holy Spirit wherever and whatever the circumstances of its teaching might be. God's Word will never return void (Isaiah 55:10,11).

7. Israel builds her third temple at last.

Perhaps in retaliation against the new "Christian movement" that has arisen by this time (after the war), or else in sheer gratitude to God for the removal of the enemies of Israel (and their mosques), the Israelis rebuild their long-destroyed temple.

The first one was built by Solomon and destroyed by Nebuchadnezzar. The second was inspired again by Haggai and Zechariah, was refurbished by King Herod, and was abounding in the days of Jesus, only to be destroyed as Christ predicted (Matthew 24:2) in A.D. 70.

Since then there have been many synagogues built around the world, including in modern

Israel, but no temple with Levitical sacrifies.

But Israelis are planning on this—that is, the orthodox Israelis. They are training young rabbis in the methods of preparing sacrifices right now in the rabbinical school in Jerusalem, not far from the present Wailing Wall or Western Wall.

They will be ready for the almost-instant rebuilding of the temple should an act of God or man destroy the mosques on the site of Mount Moriah.

Jews pray on one side of the wall and Arabs pray on the other side, at a higher elevation.

Both groups revere the site as holy. Both believe that Abraham offered his son Isaac on the spot of the Dome of the Rock Mosque, and that it was here that Solomon built his temple. The Moslems believe that Mohammed went to heaven on a white horse from this spot.

Today the orthodox Israelis want their temple, but no one in Israel would advocate it publicly today because of the Mosque of the Arabs that is on the site.

During the war the mosques will certainly be destroyed, thus opening the door for the temple to be rebuilt.

According to some researchers today, the materials have already been secured and are merely waiting for that joyous time.

Scriptural support for the fact of the rebuilding of the temple abounds.

> *And there was given me a reed like unto a rod; and the angel stood saying, Rise and*

> *measure the temple of God, and the altar,
> and those that worship therein. But the court
> which is outside the temple leave out, and
> measure it not, for it is given unto the Gen-
> tiles; and the Holy City shall they tread
> underfoot forty-two months* (Revelation
> 11:1,2).

After the oil war the Jews will rebuild the temple. Sacrificial worship involving blood sacrifices
will be instituted again after nearly two thousand
years without them.

But after the temple has been built and has
flourished for some time (perhaps several years),
the Antichrist will take over the temple and end
the sacrifices as he sets up an image of himself in
the Holy of Holies.

Two verses in Daniel (11:31 and 12:11) tell us that
the temple will be rebuilt and that the Antichrist
will take it under his control as he ends the temple
sacrificial worship. Further elaboration on this is
given in Matthew 24:15, 2 Thessalonians 2:3,4, and
Revelation 13:1-18.

8. Israel flees to Petra—the wilderness of Jor-dan.

Several Scriptural references refer to Israel flee-
ing to the wilderness, and that this wilderness will
be in Jordan.

From a geographical point of view, Jordan of today would seem a natural choice, since it is close to
Jerusalem and is right across the Jordan River (35

miles away). The terrain makes for excellent hiding except in wintertime.

However, it also seems apparent that there will be a large number of Jews who remain in Israel and live under the jurisdiction of the new Man of Sin.

Perhaps many of them will accept him as their new political messiah. That will not be hard to do, inasmuch as his companion in crime is a miracle worker and will claim to have saved Israel from the Soviets and Arabs.

Perhaps hundreds of thousands of Jews will flee when they see the abomination set up in the temple, much to their dismay.

The fact that this prediction is written in the New Testament also lends credence to the fact that the 144,000 chosen Jews will help interpret this to the orthodox Jews at the time. They will understand it clearly as they read the New Testament every day.

The Orthodox Jews, though not believing in Christ as their Messiah, will be just as adamantly opposed to the new false messiah.

They will despise him and his miracles and will cling to the truth that the true Messiah must come in the clouds of the sky, as Zechariah predicted in chapters 12 and 14 of his great prophecy. This is what the Orthodox Jews cling to till this day.

Having been to Petra several times, I found it entirely possible that this is the place in which God will feed and protect the Israelis as they flee from the Antichrist and hide in the caves and mountains of this rock fortress. It is virtually impregnable by land, and airplanes would have difficulty in scoring direct hits on the inhabitants because they would be protected by large expanses of mountain rock.

Petra was known to Solomon and Moses. Aaron was buried nearby. Traditionally the rock that Moses struck, from which water flowed, is at the entrance of Petra's caves. This entrance is a long, narrow trail that leads inside. It is passable only on foot or by camel or horse, and could easily be defended with little artillery.

9. Many Israelis will be murdered by the Anti-christ.

In the prophecies of John in Revelation chapter 12, after the woman flees into the wilderness to be fed and preserved by God for 42 months, the Antichrist (after pursuing them like Pharoah of old) is turned back in defeat.

He then returns to Judea and proceeds to murder many Jews who are left behind in retaliation for those who have escaped.

> *And the dragon was wroth with the woman, and went to make war with the remnant of her seed, which keep the commandments of God and have the testimony of Jesus Christ* (Revelation 12:17).

Not all will escape, for one reason or another.

Here in this prophecy two classes of Jews are selected for murder by war: "those that keep the commandments" (Orthodox Jews) and "those who have the testimony of Jesus" (Christian Jews).

> *And it was given unto him to make war with the saints, and to overcome them; and power was given him over all kindreds and tongues and nations* (Revelation 13:7).

No more dreaded verse could be imagined for believers living at this time. The Antichrist is hell-bent and hell-motivated to destroy the works of God. The allusion here is that he is given power over all the world, including North America.

By this time he will have taken over all of Europe. He had the ten nations of Western Europe in his power to begin with, giving him authority to act. Then came Eastern Europe and the Middle East under his jurisdiction in the wars, thus ensuring takeovers (Daniel 11:40-43).

He takes over the wealth of the world through the control of food, gold, and oil (Daniel 11:40-44); Revelation 13:1-18).

He becomes the initiator of the new world money—the international credit card on the back of the right hand or forehead (probably only seen by infrared lamps, so that no one could see your personalized number).

10. Israel is besieged by armies against the Anti-christ, who lives there. The armies come from the Far East.

By this time the Antichrist is on the throne of his false messiahship in the temple in Jerusalem. He has enacted his unified monetary system, which will be discussed later in this book.

Russia is crushed. Africa, Europe, the Middle East oil nations, North America, South America, New Zealand, and Australia will be under the Antichrist's jurisdiction.

He is enjoying world control, with only one thorn in his flesh—the rising lands of the rising sun—the Orientals.

Suddenly:

> *Tidings out of the east and out of the north shall trouble him; therefore he shall go forth with fury to destroy and utterly to make away many* (Daniel 11:44).

This is the only reference in the Old Testament to the Far East and its rising to fight the Antichrist. General statements are frequently made that nations will surround Israel and Jerusalem, but this is a definite indication of where many of the antagonists will come from.

John the Revelator says a little more:

> *And the sixth angel poured out his vial upon the great river Euphrates; and the water thereof was dried up, that the way of the kings of the east might be prepared. . . . And he gathered them together into a place called in the Hebrew tongue Armageddon* (Revelation 16:12,16).

The reference is to the bloody Battle of Armageddon. Here it is revealed that the Orientals will be coming en masse across the Euphrates River when it is miraculously dried up.

They hate the white man now in Communist China. Since Mao Tse-tung began in 1929 to overthrow the pro-Western regime of Chinese under Chiang Kaishek until he died in the 70's, he inundated China's one billion people with anti-American, anti-Western world philosophy and hatred.

We are imperialist dogs to be used and then done away with. They can have industrial cohabitation with us, and then, when we have succeeded in building them up industrially, militarily, and economically, they will turn on us and destroy the empires of the West.

This was the teaching of Mao. His successors are teaching in the same vein, though more veiled at the moment.

Economic adultery with Western nations is justified until they can rise and snuff us out.

This will be Armageddon.

God will put in their hearts to fulfill His will (Revelation 17:17).

We are building them now with oil, chemicals, industry, etc. They are being modernized and constructed with American and European expertise and training.

The battle will rage across Asia first, with smaller nations capitulating to and/or joining mighty China.

India may or may not join China. If she elects to fight, she will lose, for China will march across Asia into the Middle East for the final part of the battle.

China will not believe that it is the final part of the battle, but merely a step on the road to world control.

It is very conceivable that the entire Western world will be under the control of the Antichrist, with his headquarters in Jerusalem.

China and her Communist hordes could well feel that to win in Jerusalem is to win the world, for this will be the world capital at that time via the dictatorial regime of the Man of Sin.

To win in Israel means that the authority of the white man is dead and gone forever.

It will be a battle to end all battles, and Israel will be in the heat of it again.

11. They see the second coming—Jews first, with the Christians, then the enemies of Christ!

> *For as the lightning cometh out of the east and shineth even unto the west, so shall also the coming of the Son of man be* (Matthew 24:27).

> *Immediately after the tribulation of those days shall the sun be darkened, and the moon shall not give her light, and the stars shall fall from heaven, and the powers of the*

> *heavens shall be shaken. And then shall appear the sign of the Son of Man in heaven; and then shall all the tribes of the earth mourn, and they shall see the Son of Man coming in the clouds of heaven with power and great glory* (Matthew 24:29,30).

Israel weeps when the Messiah comes at last!

Why the weeping? Because they at last see who it is that the Son of Man is—none other than the Lord Jesus Christ, who was crucified on the cross for their sins and ours.

> *And it shall come to pass in that day that I will seek to destroy all the nations that come against Jerusalem. And I will pour upon the house of David and upon the inhabitants of Jerusalem the spirit of grace and supplications; and they shall look upon me whom they have pierced, and they shall mourn for him as one mourneth for his only son, and shall be in bitterness for him as one that is in bitterness for his firstborn* (Zechariah 12:9,10).

Zechariah 12:11-14 further amplifies this theme. They recognize Him and rejoice inwardly that He has come, but are ashamed at the treatment He received at their hands, as it is thoroughly revealed to them by God who the real Messiah is—the Son of the carpenter in Nazareth of 2000 years ago. This means to them that the New Testament was right and they were dead wrong!

The Spirit of God moves upon them, and nationally they accept Christ. The greatest revival of all comes first to the house of Israel.

> *And his feet shall stand in that day upon the Mount of Olives, which is before Jerusalem on the east. And the Mount of Olives shall cleave in the midst thereof toward the east and toward the west, and there shall be a very great valley; and half the mountain will be removed toward the north, and half of it toward the south. . . . And in that day shall living waters go out from Jerusalem: half of them toward the Former Sea and half of them toward the Hinder Sea; in summer and winter shall it be. And the Lord shall be King over all the earth; in that day shall there be one Lord, and his name one* (Zechariah 14:4,8,9).

The Jews will open their hearts to the Lord, and He will establish His kingdom forever, with His headquarters in Jerusalem.

This is also the end of the Battle of Armageddon (to be discussed in more detail later) and the beginning of the 1000 years of perfect peace—the millennial reign predicted in the amazing prophecies of the Bible.

The Jewish torture is over. They are never again to be divided, and the land of Israel will become their home forever.

3

Shockwaves from Europe

Europe is presented in Biblical prophecy as—

Ten toes on a man's foot (Daniel 2)

Ten horns on an ugly, indescribable beast —Rome (Daniel 7)

Ten horns sitting next to seven heads on a beast with the body of a leopard—the Antichrist (Revelation 13)

Ten horns on a beast with seven heads supporting a whore on its back who is killed (Revelation 17)

(The woman is the false church on the back of the Antichrist supporting her for a time.)

The nations of Europe are referred to in this way only in the prophecies of Daniel and Revelation.

Two words in Ezekiel appear to represent Europe also: Gomer and Togarmah. These were originally the grandsons of Noah, through

Japheth, who became mighty nations representing geographical areas of that time and of today.

FROM THE EUROPEAN PROPHECIES
WE LEARN THE FOLLOWING FACTS:

1. Ten nations will arise in united power out of the old Roman Empire. Only ten nations, and not the whole Roman Empire will be revived (Daniel 7:23,24).

2. A presumably European or Middle Eastern personality will be selected from these ten nations to take their reins of government and be their elected leader (Daniel 8).

3. They will give their complete military, economic, and political power to this dictator (Revelation 17:13).

4. Three of these ten nations will oppose this leader eventually, but he will subdue them (Daniel 7:20).

5. They will retain their power with this leader, but only for a very short time (Revelation 17:12).

6. He will turn on them and usurp complete control, in dictatorial fashion (Revelation 17:9-13).

7. He will use their powers given to him to issue an edict of protection to Israel for seven years (Daniel 9:27).

8. He will turn against his European home and will march on Israel halfway into the seven-year period (Daniel 11:40-45).

9. They will all work in cooperation with the false church, which is any church that denies the deity of Christ and the value of the blood of Christ as the only way to salvation (Revelation 17:1-18).

10. The leader will use them to eventually destroy this church (Revelation 17:16).

11. These nations who support him will be destroyed at Christ's second coming (Revelation 19).

Everything that is happening in Europe today and in countries around the world with respect to Europe's prestige and Gross National Product is pushing us into the final prophecies for this area of the world.

The amazing Biblical prophecies clearly reveal that ten nations will arise, and it is entirely possible that the current ten nations embraced in the European Common Market are the ten referred to in Daniel 2 and 7.

Italy, France, West Germany, Luxembourg, Holland, Belgium, England, Denmark, Ireland, and Greece constitute the present European community.

In 1948, the year Israel became a nation, the nations started to form, and after a few years there were ten nations. but Norway dropped out, leaving nine.

Greece is a nation that could play an important role in producing the Antichrist, according to Daniel 8.

But the first indication of prophecy teaching us of Europe's participation comes in Daniel 2, where King Nebuchadnezzar had a dream involving many nations.

He did not remember the dream, but finally Daniel revealed it to the king as God revealed it to him.

The king had dreamed of an image of a man. The head was of gold, the chest of silver, the thighs of brass, the two legs of iron, and the feet and toes of iron and clay.

Daniel revealed to the king what the dream meant, as God told him to.

The head of gold was Babylon and the current government of the king himself.

The chest of silver was the Medes and Persians, who would eventually conquer the Babylonians.

The thighs of brass represented the Greeks under Alexander the Great.

The final part of the main body was the legs of iron, representing Rome.

Then came the ten toes of iron and clay, a bad mixture that had a difficult time holding together. Daniel revealed that the ten toes were kingdoms that would not cleave to one another, though they would try and would be united in some ways.

> *Whereas thou sawest the feet and toes, part of potter's clay and part of iron, the kingdom shall be divided; but there shall be in it the strength of the iron, forasmuch as thou sawest the iron mixed with clay. And as the toes of the feet were part of iron and part of clay, so the kingdom shall be partly strong and partly broken. And whereas thou sawest iron mixed with miry clay, they shall mingle themselves with the seed of men; but they shall not cleave one to another, even as iron is not mixed with clay* (Daniel 2:41-43).

This is certainly true of the nations involved today. England is certainly not cleaving to Ireland.

Italy has been politically a clay nation, with over 40 governments in 35 years, and very weakened currency.

West Germany is extremely strong, with a stronger GNP than the U.S. Her currency is the strongest in the world, partly due to conservative government policies and partly due to being heavily backed by gold in the government's coffers.

France has been strong in certain areas. Belgium is the home of the NATO headquarters and the Common Market organization itself.

These nations are both large and small, and are varied in their ways of life and standards of living.

They have fought one another for centuries, and for the ten of them to finally pull together and form a parliament of Europe is a miracle of modern-day diplomacy—or is it that God put this unity into their hearts in order to fulfill His will? Certainly it is the latter.

They have programs covering all efforts of agreement, from agriculture to energy to military aspirations.

More recently, under West Germany's leadership (in cooperation with France) they have enacted legislation producing ECU—the European Currency Unit.

It is a monetary unit not yet in actual printed creation, but is considered a European Monetary System that:

1. Could take the place of the U.S. dollar as the world's reserve currency. That is, it could become the currency by which all products will be priced (indexed) and into whose currency all other nations will have to exchange theirs in order to buy internationally for commerce and trade.
2. Is backed by 20 percent or more of solid gold reserves. (The dollar is no longer backed by gold.)
3. Is backed by a growing GNP in Europe by all the participating nations.
4. Is used on the international level for all

purchases between the nations involved with it.

5. Will be in print within two years, according to late reports.

6. Is symbolical of the mark-of-the-Beast credit card coming by the Antichrist, as it is the first united monetary unit ever agreed on by nations anywhere. (ECU is not evil and is not related to 666, but it does show us how this will come about as a united monetary system for the nations of the world under the Antichrist.)

How long after the ten nations unite politically will it be until the Antichrist takes over the nations and makes them his own?

The answer is unknown, but it could take some time, perhaps several years or perhaps only a matter of months.

In Daniel 2 we might see a period of time during which they "mingle with the seed of men." This evidently means with other nations, for they are already mingling with one another.

This could well mean a period of time during this decade of the 80's when Europe will rise to such prominence as to be the leader in the affairs of men, rather than the United States.

The timing implication is that it could take time for them to realize their weaknesses and their strengths, and then in utter futility they will turn to the leader and ask him to bring about greater unification.

Timing in prophecy is always a dangerous pursuit. We dare not presume to know it all.

With today's rapidly changing world economic scene, along with political maneuverings and mighty military powers rising, these changes could take place fairly soon after the ten nations unite.

EUROPE WILL BE THE SCENE OF MOST OF THE ACTIONS OF THE ANTICHRIST FOR HIS FIRST PERIOD OF POWER

The Europeans, in their quest for world power as a world government, need a leader who is both charismatic and prudent, and has enough military and economic experience coupled with political expertise to lead them through the modern maze of economic and military complexities of this tough hour.

Disunity reigns periodically in today's European parliament of the ten nations.

They have relied too much on the United States for protection from the Soviet forces, known as the Warsaw Pact Forces. (The reason for this title is that the amalgamation of fighting forces of the Communist bloc of Eastern European nations met in Warsaw to form this military alliance.)

Currently it is the Warsaw Pact Forces that are far ahead of the NATO (North Atlantic Treaty Organization) forces of the West, led by the United States in fighting men.

EUROPE AND THE COMING OIL WAR

It appears that the Soviets will attack on the European front as well as in the Middle East, according to the best interpretations of Daniel 11:40,41:

> And at the time of the end shall the king of south push at him; and the king of the north shall come against him like a whirlwind, with chariots and with horsemen and with many ships; and he shall enter into the countries, and shall overflow and pass over. He shall enter also into the glorious land, and many countries shall be overthrown.

The Antichrist first reigns in Europe—the Western European theater, to be exact.

The Soviets have not yet attacked, according to this passage.

While the Antichrist is still tying things together and building his vast empire and new-world government from the "iron and clay" countries of the Western sector, the Soviets and their satellites attack him.

Europe could be inundated with war and devastation until the Soviets are destroyed.

We will go into detail on this subject in our next chapter, but for now it will suffice to suggest that Europe will be attacked and savagely involved in this war.

EUROPE AND THE GREAT WHORE OF REVELATION

The great whore, who sits on a scarlet-colored beast with seven heads and ten horns, who is clothed with purple and scarlet color and is decked with gold, precious stones, and pearls, and who holds a golden cup in her hand, is a mystery indeed.

Much has been written about her, but we interpret her to be a composite of all false religions that deny the power of the blood of Christ as the only atoning work of God to expiate our sins.

The great whore has "sat upon many waters" and has committed adultery with the "kings of the earth."

She represents all the evil in all religions that deceive human beings, from the beginning of false religion until this time.

Satan obviously has those who follow him in their hearts who are not religious. They are totally secular, worldly, and not inclined toward any type of faith.

But he also has his religious followers. They belong to many churches, groups, sects, organizations, etc. Many of them are there for the religious feeling they receive. They truly believe that theirs is the right way, but they are truly wrong. They are sincere, but that is no criterion for gaining salvation or getting into the kingdom of heaven.

Others are part of religious organizations for a

multiplicity of reasons. With some it is just good fun, good business, and a place to make friends.

Evil religions have their following out of fear, or out of the sheer devilishness of the acts of worship. Some of these include rituals of bloodletting of humans and of animals.

Religions in India, where I have been, are religions where sincere people worship in monkey temples or sex temples.

I have seen them bowing down to kiss or feed filthy monkeys, firmly believing that they have powers to aid them spiritually.

Millions of others worship the images of the sex organs of men and women. I have watched as they worshiped, hoping this would make them fertile, sexual, greater.

There are religions where outsiders are to see nothing or learn nothing of their initiation rites, as they cut, bleed, wound, and maim the initiates.

Animals are worshiped, humans are worshiped, and nature is worshiped—all of which is described in the eternal classic words of Paul in Romans:

> For the invisible things of God from the creation of the world are clearly seen, being understood by the things that are made, even his eternal power and Godhead, so that they [humans] are without excuse, because that, when they knew God, they glorified him not as God, neither were thankful, but became vain in their imaginations, and their foolish

> *heart was darkened. Professing themselves to be wise, they became fools, and changed the glory of the incorruptible God into an image made like corruptible man, and to birds and fourfooted beasts and creeping things. Wherefore God also gave them up to uncleanness through the lusts of their own hearts, to dishonor their own bodies between themselves, who changed the truth of God into a lie, and worshiped and served the creature more than the Creator, who is blessed forever. Amen* (Romans 1:20-25).

The human race had the truth but turned from the truth, and now they are suffering because of a lack of the truth as it was revealed in the Old and New Testaments.

This great whore represents all religions who have departed from the way of truth in Jesus Christ.

To make her represent just one organization or one great or small denomination would be to destroy the teaching intended.

She represents all who have followed Satan in false religions, regardless of what they think about the truthfulness of their so-called faiths.

God calls her Babylon. This is intriguing and is not the only time God uses the term Babylon in the Scriptures.

It is usually used in a derogatory manner, indicating that God is against whatever and whomever He is describing by this term.

Babylon is the worst term used in the Bible for nations, people, or things on earth that God is very angry with.

Babylon sums up all the wickedness, rebellion, evil, corruption, or theological error in one name. This name "Babylon" means to God all that is evil in the name of religion on the earth.

Babylon certainly involves Europe, and in this particular era of time and area of location it is apparently supported by the Antichrist during the first years of his rise to power as a world leader in Europe.

He supports the false church but persecutes the true church.

Babylon finally comes to her end. It is by one evil destroying another. In order to facilitate the rise of the Antichrist as a personage to worship, claiming that he is the Messiah, he has her destroyed by the ten nations that he controls.

> And the ten horns which thou sawest upon the beast, these shall hate the whore and shall make her desolate and naked, and shall eat her flesh and burn her with fire (Revelation 17:16).

Political powers turn on recognized religions of all kinds and destroy them through military power and legislative power.

The religions of the nations, small and large, important and unimportant, will be legislated out of business. The legislation will be enforced, unquestionably at great bloodshed, for even these false faiths have their devoted followers.

The great whore will die a horrible death, in the will of God, as He uses evil to crush evil.

Europe will be the headquarters for this evil, and the scene of her demise. Great persecution and bloodshed will result during this period, which could take over a year.

WILL THE FALSE PROPHET COME OUT OF EUROPE OR THE MIDDLE EAST?

There is little in Scripture to indicate the answer. In all probability the False Prophet, who is the right arm and public relations director for the Antichrist, will rise from Europe, as more than one nation will be involved in his efforts to push the regime of the Antichrist.

It does seem reasonable to assume that this False Prophet could be a European and will work with the Antichrist to establish his credibility throughout Europe and the Middle East.

It is also possible that he could be from the Middle East, for according to the prophecies of Revelation 13:15-18 his primary effort may well be in the land of Israel, as he leads Jews into an acceptance of the Antichrist as the new Messiah by putting his image in the new temple and causing it to have miraculous powers of communication, etc.

That there will be a partner-in-crime is no doubt. The Antichrist will be assisted by this man, who causes all to worship the Antichrist by his miraculous powers.

He will be totally unchristian and unorthodox as far as the Christian and Judaistic religions and philosophies are concerned.

He will be destroyed by Jesus Christ simultaneously with the Antichrist as Christ returns at the Battle of Armageddon (Revelation 19:11-21).

CURRENT INTRIGUING EVENTS TRANSPIRING IN EUROPE LEAD US TO THE FULFILLMENT OF THE AMAZING PROPHECIES OF THE BIBLE

The nine nations have invited Greece to be nation number ten. She accepted in 1981.

The parliaments of Europe are attempting to form a united currency called ECU-European Currency Unit.

It is backed by 20 percent gold; that is, the nations participating must have 20 percent of their national reserves in their treasuries and central banks in gold in order to participate. This elevates gold as true money.

This united monetary system was adopted in March 1979 and is implemented now. A commemorative coin was introduced in December 1979 indicating that the new money was in power as a monetary unit being used on the international level for commerce and trade rather than merely on the local, man-on-the-street level.

When calling the European Common Market

representatives in Washington, D.C., I was informed that they do not intend on making the money available to all the members of the ten nations presently, but that eventually it could become the united currency of the people of Europe.

They stated that they felt it would be readily accepted by all nations as equal amounts were distributed to everyone according to his wealth and that his property would be valued accordingly, without anyone suffering loss financially by the trade-in of the old monies for the new.

The unifying power of the monetary system would tie all the nations of Western Europe together so tightly that nothing could separate them.

This monetary union will pave the way for the mark-of-the-Beast credit card, to be discussed later in this book.

Watch for the military buildup of Western Europe's forces as the U.S. pulls out support piece by piece.

According to Bible prophecy, Europe must build its own military power to a point of world-accepted expertise. They will, and they are now. Currently the great generals of Europe say they are not ready for conflict with the Soviet forces. Word has it from reliable Western European and NATO leaders that if the Soviets were to attack right now, they would overrun Europe within two weeks because of their superior conventional and nuclear power.

They are ahead of us ten to one in tanks and men. Special missiles have the power and aim to knock out our retaliation missiles as they engage in a strike-first operation against us.

The establishment of ECU could bring about the death of the U.S. dollar and the collapse of our stock market and total economy.

If the Arabs, who hold many billions of American petrodollars (dollars paid for oil) decide for one emotional reason or another (and they have many of them to choose from right now) to dump the dollars for gold, silver, and/or ECU from Europe, then we are in serious trouble in the United States.

Dumping the dollars for the Arabs would be a face-saving move that they would require if:

A. Israel does not give up the West Bank of the Jordan Valley to the Palestinians after much Arab rhetoric and demands.

B. Jerusalem is not included in this handover of land to the PLO.

C. The Khoumeni drums up support by the Shiite Moslems to help him from all over the Middle East and North Africa. He has power over these nations via the Shiite Moslem population. They are a minority, but that fact only makes them fight harder. The Sunni Moslems are the most popular throughout the Moslem world, but this does not mean they are always in power.

If dollars are dumped on the international monetary exchange for any of these reasons (or new reasons that may come any day), there could be an overnight depression in the United States, with too many dollars hitting the country overnight.

Our inflation has irritated our Western European allies as well as the nations of OPEC. They are all getting (as we) less and less for each dollar they spend from the products they sell us.

For over 40 years the dollar has been the world's reserve currency. Since we aided Europe and Japan after World War Two with billions of dollars, all products of the world were and are indexed (priced) in dollars rather than yen, marks, francs, etc.

The dollar won this honor as no other money has in world history because of the greatness of the United States under the free-enterprise system.

But now, with rampant inflation facing us and a government not able to cope with it, we have nations around the world worried that they are holding too many dollars, and nations considering how to get rid of them without hurting themselves or us.

ECU came as a direct result of the leaders of West Germany and France wearying of the dying dollar and not willing to let the economies of their respective countries falter with ours.

West Germany's Chancellor Helmut Schmidt stated that they were not going to fall along with the United States by holding to their U.S. money any longer.

ECU came into existence to help Europe fight against the dollar as the world's reserve currency.

It is possible that ECU will become the world's reserve currency, held by all nations as Europe rises and the United States recedes as a world power.

If the Arabs dump dollars, and if the Europeans do the same in the headlong rush (once it starts) to save their necks and get as much for their dollars as possible at the same time as other nations start dumping them, then the United States will have a depression.

Such a depression, brought about by Arabs and Western Europeans, would make 1929 and the 1930's look small by economic comparisons.

The hardships will be much worse.

In 1929 the government had much gold to pay for goods from overseas. Now we have little gold.

In 1929 the government was not in the disarray that it is now, with the people having little or no confidence in it to govern the nation and sustain its currency. What would be the case if we fell into a terrible depression now?

In 1929 neither Europe nor the Arab nations were dumping billions of dollars on the foreign exchange markets. Now they will.

The dollar will have no chance for immediate recovery. It will be a hyperinflationary blowoff!

It will be the opposite problem to 1929, when the

Federal Reserve System stopped the presses and we had deflation of the currency. There was not enough currency in the general marketplace of the nation to keep business circulating, producing, growing, and developing.

When you have money in the marketplace of the nation, you have a growing nation. Business thrives, manufacturers produce, and the economy grows as consumers have money with which to buy. Demand determines supply. Suppliers need what is known in economics as "liquidity in the marketplace."

Currently we have *illiquidity* in the marketplace. High interest rates, forced on us by the Fed, cause this illiquidity. Thus we have a terrible slowdown in business throughout America today. We are in recession. If it does not ease, we will be in a terrible depression.

Illiquidity—no money in the marketplaces of the nation—kills business, produces unemployment, reduces the nation's capital, cuts consumer buying, and places the whole nation under a terrrible strain that only liquidity can alleviate. And that will take time, even after interest rates lower.

When too much power (interest-rate power) has been placed in the hands of powers outside the government, who are private concerns and have much to gain by their own self-serving judgments and decisions, this is wrong for the nation involved.

In this nation we have a set of circumstances

related to events catapulting in on us from Western Europe.

In 1913 the Federal Reserve System was instituted in this country by the great perseverance of European bankers, who had tried for decades to make sure that America had a central bank for the creation and management of its money supply, *apart from the federal government itself.*

This was established after years of political maneuverings, machinations, and trickery. Congress, in a sense, abrogated its responsibility to coin, manage, and distribute money by delegating it to the private owners of the Federal Reserve System. That's right—private owners. This is documented and available to you in the material that will be suggested for your further enlightenment on this shocking subject.

They have the power to coin money as they see fit. The federal government is on one side, and the Federal Reserve System is on the other. In the middle, acting as liaison, is the Federal Reserve Board, partially appointed by the government and partially controlled by the Federal Reserve System.

They determine the money supply for the nation. They do this in collaboration with the government.

This is called "macroeconomics," for it is economics on the large scale. (You at your home engage in "microeconomics" every time you attempt to balance your personal or family budget in this critical hour of inflation.)

With the present government budget of about a billion dollars and growing every year, we have to have a tremendous money supply to keep up with it.

The government gets money in three ways:

A. Taxes.
B. T-bills; government paper certificates offered to banks, savings and loans, corporations, etc.; various government bonds at a high rate of interest that will be paid back with our money later on.
C. More printed money by the Fed. Oddly enough, when the government needs money, it prints bonds. The Fed creates the money. They exchange bonds for bills (or credit money) from one another. The government gets the credit money or the actual money bills, and the Fed gets the bonds. The Fed then can sell the bonds to any of about 21 bond-dealing houses in New York City and pocket the money made on the interest with the bonds!

No book on Biblical prophecy would be complete without discussing the financial system controlling the Western-world nations.

No doubt Satan had three plans to control the world and defeat the plans of God for Christ's millennial reign on earth.

One plan was to fill the earth with heathenism.

One-third of the world is now in heathenism, in spite of mass missionary movements.

The second plan was to cover the more intelligent areas of the earth with Communism. This succeeded to the extent that about one-third of the world is now under Communism.

But how would Satan conquer the evangelical world? How could he get to the hotbeds of Christianity and the more educated and industrialized nations enjoying the free-enterprise system?

One-third of the world's people were and are under heatenism. One-third are under Communism. The remaining third would be conquered through godless commercialism.

Heathenism, Communism, commercialism. The last of these would have to come by defeating people where they had their greatest power—in money.

But the seeds of monetary defeat would have to be planted early in order to bring about the eventual demise of the nations, as Satan planned it.

He would have his one-world government and his man to run a world of socialism.

That has already been planned. Now, to carry it out, international bankers were used to bring about central controlling banks in each of the Western nations.

These central banks would control the money supply, and yet, because they were given this power by the legislative branches of each nation's governments, they would have to act in concert with the governments for a time in order to bring about confidence and greater control—control that eventually would bring the greatest and most Christian nations on earth under Satan's power when he was ready for it.

He is ready now. Socialism is rising.

Most of the nations of the Western world are controlled in their money supply by central banks, all of which are hooked up to one another in Europe and to each of the nations, including New Zealand, Australia, Canada, and the United States, as well as the nations of Europe, Africa, Israel, etc.

The seeds of our own destruction are planted within the very monetary system that seemed to give birth to the free-enterprise system and the growth of the nations of the Western world.

In order for the U.S. to ever join Europe's one-world government, we would have to experience the death of our dollar, our sovereignty, and our government for the most part.

The mechanics of government may stay intact, but the power to govern would shift to Europe if the nation were on its knees in a deep depression and Europe offered immediate alternatives to millions of suffering Americans.

How do you bring a nation to its knees after three centuries of prosperity? Control its money supply and interest rates. Let the men doing so be convinced that they are doing the nation and the world a favor by bringing us all together under one world banner for the good of all mankind.

Many who espouse this philosophy believe that it will do away with all opposing ideologies, wars, shortages of products, hunger, famine, and inequities in the earth.

If one world government controls all oil, food, and money, could they not bring about equitable distribution of food, energy, and money? Yes, they could if it were heaven. But that will come later.

Even Abraham Lincoln fought the central bank to his death, and stated that only over his dead body would the government give this power to private money brokers. He died. The brokers pushed on and won.

One last thought on central banks and Europe. Just outside Culpepper, Virginia, is a large and ominous building that was recently completed. It is a central computer house, hooking up the U.S. banking establishment with the computerized banking system of Europe.

Now all banks in the world can be linked together. All records can be on microfilm, and world central banking will be a grand possibility.

Through sophisticated electronic computerization, all monies paid you could be done through computer digital inputs. Your earnings will be direct-deposited by your firm, without the exchange of checks, money, etc.

This would save millions of hours as well as billions of lost or stolen dollars, and it all sounds very sensible.

Every business establishment from gas stations

to grocery stores would have access to use this central computer control. When you go to buy anything, it would indicate your balance without human help or interference. It would be done by computerized control.

You would be issued your own computer number for identification when shopping.

The next step?

Read on.

4

Shockwaves from the Soviet Union

Magog is the prophetical term for the nation we know as Russia, and now today with its broader appellation, the Soviet Union.

Many people are part of the Soviet Union who want you to know they are not Russians. Many nations or former nations make up the Soviets, including over 40 million Moslems in the southern region.

From the early 1930's, after the rise of Communism in Russia took place, the Russians engaged in expansionistic tactics and took over many areas. Estonia, Latvia, and Lithuania fell to Russian conquests.

Since that time more of Eastern Europe has fallen to Communist expansionism, involving Czechoslovakia, Poland, Hungary, East Germany, East Berlin, etc. Now they have planted their Marxist philosophy firmly in Angola, Libya, Ethiopia, and Afghanistan. They are moving in a sinister way toward many other areas of the world, using every tactic available to them, including the export of Communist-trained Castroites from Cuba to expand Communism throughout the world,

South Yemen, on the Persian Gulf, is virtually controlled by Cubans. They are exporting revolution throughout the African states of Liberia and Rhodesia via their puppet governments there.

The entire Caribbean Sea area is falling into puppet Communist governments as island after island falls to "people's governments."

This is dangerous indeed to the vital import lifeline to the United States, since so much oil and minerals travel this route from the southern tip of Africa up through the South Atlantic, through the Caribbean Sea to ports in the United States or ports in the Caribbean area, where giant oil tankers unload their oil to be refined and then shipped on to the U.S. on the West and East coasts of the nation.

The U.S. is unable to receive some of the largest oil tankers that have been built in recent years. These giant cargo ships dock at Caracao and Trinidad to unload to smaller ships or refineries owned and operated by the multinational oil barons, to be shipped to the U.S. later.

Lenin, father of the Bolshevik revolution that swept Russia from 1917 to 1923 and finally won the nation, stated in 1923 that Communism would conquer the world.

He stated that he had a five-point program to cover the earth with Communism. The points were:

1. Take over as much of Eastern Europe as possible with Communism. They did as indicated.

2. Take over the Far East with Communism in China and the lesser nations of Asia. They have done this and are continuing to do it. We all know of Mao Tse-tung and his Communist revolution over the mainland of China, though he finally turned against Russia. Vietnam, Cambodia, Laos, North Korea, and other areas where Communism has expanded are fresh in our minds, fulfilling this prophecy.

3. Take over as much of Africa and the Suez Canal as possible.

4. Take over Central America, the Caribbean Sea area, and the Panama Canal as soon as possible. The Panama Canal is now in the hands of a Marxist government. The Caribbean is falling like dominoes. In nation after nation revolutions are pushing out the leaders desiring to be free and are instead promoting Communists to power. Some of these are in the very areas that our ships have to come through to deliver vital goods to the U.S.

5. Finally, conquer the United States by surrounding her with vast military powers, cutting off her vital shipping lanes, and disrupting her energy and mineral sup-

ply. Until this can be done, work with
the free world in order gain loans, goods,
and scientific expertise for Soviet use until they are through with the financial cohabitation with the West.

Could all of this really happen?

Yes. Russia has moved into the Middle East almost overnight, and from one end of the area to
the other is a growing menace to the United States,
Israel, and our allies who need oil energy around
the world.

Russia has advanced on and taken over Afghanistan, with over 80,000 crack troops in that land of
Moslems next to Iran's oil fields in the middle of
the Persian Gulf.

Russia has advanced on and taken over Afghanistan, with over 80,000 crack troops in that land of
less adults in Kibbutzim and city streets and farm
lanes seems to be their specialty. They especially
like to attack when all are sleeping soundly with
no guards or guns.

Just a little of the billions of dollars of oil money
which the Arab nations have earned by the sale of
oil could have built two or three lovely modern
cities in Jordan or Lebanon or Syria for these
refugees and made them live like normal human
beings, instead of forcing them to live in the hovels
of mud currently housing them.

Little has been done by the rich Arab oil world
for these helpless pawns in the game, except what
has been done through the United Nations Refugee

Department in feeding and helping them. Much of this has come from the United States and her friends, such as Canada, etc.

For over 32 years the refugees have waited and died in the germ-infested areas they are living in.

The Israeli government has done much to help them, rebuild them, and encourage them.

Over 450,000 Palestinians have dual passports and live in Israel currently. They have Israeli and Palestinian passports, allowing them the privilege of being like an Israeli citizen and yet remaining ethnically Arab and living as Moslems.

The Israelis have built areas for them and given them running water, electricity, etc.

Schools have been built and Arab governments have been set up for governing themselves in these communities, although the policing is done by the Israelis themselves.

Bethlehem is all Arab and is run by Arabs in their city government. I have met and talked with the Mayor more than once. Naturally he would like Palestinian rule rather than Israeli rule, but so would the Hungarians and Czechs and Poles—all conquered people. But no one says anything about them anymore.

Nazareth is an Arab city with Arab leadership. Having had dinner with the Mayor and other Arab leaders in this community, I know how well off they are. They live well and have security and privileges not accorded many of their peers in other Arab countries. The Israeli government does much for these Arab leaders and their people.

Arabs live much better in Bethlehem and Nazareth than they do in Cairo and Damascus.

These ancient Arab cities are filthy by comparison, and the privileges of the people cannot be compared with their counterparts in Israel.

One of the worst nights and times of my life I spent in Damascus. The overnight hotel was very dirty, and I felt extremely unsafe. This was one of the best hotels there, but it was an antique.

Arab animosity was never stronger against Israel than when I was in Damascus.

I was invited by the government to come and film for television purposes concerning my lastest television series (telling about situations in the Middle East).

With government driver and liaison officer, I was filming just outside the city of Damascus at his invitation as the sun was going down one evening, when to my amazement and delight, with my large 16-millimeter camera on my shoulder, I picked up strange sights and movements nearby. They were missiles aimed at Israel and Mount Hermon, with Soviet markings. It looked like Soviets and Syrians working around them in the distance.

Somehow my telephoto lens went right in on that intriguing scene, and I got the whole layout of where the missiles were and where they were aimed.

My family and touring friends were not far away at a hotel on the Sea of Galilee, awaiting me to join them in two days on an Israeli Kibbutzim.

Suddenly, while feeling elated at my photographic find, I felt a cold steel barrel poking in my back rib cage.

Turning, I discovered not one gun, but six, all aimed at me while filming censored areas. The men were angry!

We were all arrested by the military force of Syria, which I discovered have more power than the politicians. That was a switch from American procedure!

They not being able to speak English, nor I Arabic, I was saved from talking or saying much of anything except through my Arab government guide, who emotionally gestured that this man would never film anything wrong!

They went through this for hours while I was under car arrest at the barracks and they argued on my behalf.

I felt I would land in a Syrian jail. That would be the pit of pits, for they have a very inhuman reputation on how they treat political prisoners or spies for Israel. (They were convinced I was spying and filming for Israel.)

As quickly as the ordeal began, it ended. The commander came out and said in very broken English, "I am sorry for arrest. You good man. Come again."

That was it. They let me keep my film—all of it—even as I was busily engaged in trying to destroy and hide the evidence of what I had taken.

Had they taken the time to have it developed (and they could have), that would have been evidence enough that I was indeed a spy for Israel, and anything could have happened!

I thought of the Apostle Paul just then, who escaped a garrison of soldiers by being let down in a basket by a rope over the wall. It was the same city—just a different garrison of soldiers.

According to a survey, 83 percent of all Israelis believe they are going to face the Soviets and the Arabs the next time in the bloodiest of conflagrations, and that it will happen before 1985!

Leaders in the Pentagon, Ottawa, London, Egypt, Tel Aviv, Jerusalem, New Delhi, Bonn, Rome, Paris, Brussels, etc., all believe that we are soon headed for a great military confrontation between the Western powers of democracy and the Eastern powers of brutal Communism.

Ezekiel gives us the clearest picture of this battle between the Arabs and the Jews, the East and the West.

> *And the word of the Lord came unto me, saying, Son of Man, set thy face against Gog, the land of Magog, the chief prince of Meshech and Tubal, and prophecy against him, and say, Thus saith the Lord God, behold, I am against thee, O Gog, the chief prince of Meshech and Tubal; and I will turn thee back, and put hooks into thy jaws, and I will bring thee forth, and all thine army, horses and horsemen, all of them clothed with all*

sorts of armour, even a great company with bucklers and shields, all of them handling swords: Persia, Ethiopia, and Libya with them, all of them with shields and helmet: Gomer and all his bands, the house of Togarmah of the north quarters, and all his bands, and many people with thee. . . . After many days thou shalt be visited: in the latter years thou shalt come into the land that is brought back from the sword and is gathered out of many people, against the mountains of Israel, which have been always waste; but it is brought forth out of the nations, and they shall dwell safely all of them. . . . And thou shalt say, I will go up to the land of the unwalled villages; I will go to them that are at rest, that dwell safely, all of them dwelling without walls, and having neither bars nor gates, to take a spoil, and to take a prey to turn thine hand upon the desolate places that are now inhabited, and upon the people that are gathered out of the nations. (Ezekiel 38:1-12).

"Thou shalt come from thy place out of the north parts" is another confirmation as to where Magog is coming from.

The Israeli Old Testament which is in use today in Israel indicates clearly that Magog is the land of Rosh, or Russia as we know it today.

There is no doubt in their minds who Magog is. Magog and Meshech and Tubal were brothers and the sons of Japheth, and were also the grandsons of Noah after the days of the ark.

Togarmah was the son of Gomer and the great-grandson of Noah.

These boys became men, who became mighty tribes and ultimately nations on the earth that we know of today.

The names are changed but the places are the same.

Magog became the Scythians, who became the Roshites, who became the land of Russia today.

Gomer became Eastern Europe, covering such areas as today's East Germany, Poland, Czechoslovakia, etc.

Tubal could have been the Eastern section of the land of Magog, which became the city of Tubolsk. Meshech eventually became today's Moscow.

Togarmah is what we know today as Turkey, and could even embrace (according to some early maps) the area of Syria where it joins the border of Turkey today.

Thus Magog joins forces with the politcal powers of all these geographical areas and then advances on Israel.

Currently the Soviet Union has expanded its actual political presence or ideological presence into most of these areas.

Gomer belongs to present-day Russia or the Soviet Union. East Germany has been taken by them, along with the other countries already listed as belonging to them, by the military prowess conquering in these areas.

Syria, insofar as Togarmah is part of North-western Syria (the part above Lebanon), is in tune with the Soviets currently. The Russian KGB are all over Damascus, arming the PLO, heading up political factions, and engaging in military training.

Turkey has not fallen into the Soviet camp but is ordering materials from the Soviets and fighter planes, plus ammunition, military equipment, and peace goods from their neighbor to the north.

While standing on the banks of the Bosporus in Istanbul not long ago, I could observe mighty Soviet tankers coming down from the Black Sea into the Sea of Marmora and then into the large Mediterranean Sea.

The Turkish government naturally has to cooperate with the Soviets, as they share a border together and bodies of water mutually beneficial to all concerned.

With the Common Market countries favoring the positioning of Turkey's enemy Greece into the Common Market as nation number ten, and with NATO cooperating so closely with the Common Market, it places Turkey in the strange position of wishing it could be more Western but in reality leaning eastward and northward.

Turkey is, after all, a Moslem nation, favoring Moslem decisions against the U.S., its allies, and Israel.

Religious ties are strong with the Moslem portion

of OPEC, and Turkey relies on aid from neighboring oil-producing states to some extent.

Internally, Turkey is in trouble with its leadership and monetary situation. They are in a state of high inflation and have a low Gross National Product. They are very poor people, living peasant-style, with a Moslem religion that does very little for their industrial development and relationship with the Western nations.

Religion and custom often enter into poltical relationships among nations.

Greece is more Christian in its philosophy than Turkey, and thus it fits into the world of the Common Market because of its Greek Orthodox Catholic background (more so than the Turkish Moslem faith and customs).

Togarmah is in the direct line of the Soviets as they would come south to aid the Moslem Arabs against their enemy Israel.

Turkey is now leaning toward the Soviet and Arab Moslem world more than ever, putting her right in line with the amazing prophecies of the Bible indicating that she will cooperate with the Soviet Union and the Arab states against Israel.

Once any "Holy Islamic War" breaks out, watch for the Turks to join it, as they did centuries ago against the Crusaders in the once-mighty days of the Turks and the Sultans, who attempted to rule the Middle East and conquer Christianity and Judaism.

Do not forget how the Turks treated about two

million or more Armenians. They murdered the Christian Armenians, and to this day they have holidays celebrating it.

If there is a Moslem war against Judaism and Christianity, the Turks will join them. This is the war of Ezekiel chapters 38 and 39.

These predictions indicate that Magog (Russia) will fight against Israel with all these other nations on her side, after Israel has come home and taken the land by the sword. This is precisely what has happened since 1948, when the United Nations passed resolutions allowing the Jews to return to their original land of Palestine against Arab protests.

But the Jews took the land by the power of the sword, and not by legislative negotiations.

It has been more than three decades of war—war that has cost thousands of lives on all sides.

Every able-bodied man in Israel is in the Israeli armed forces either as a regular soldier or a reserve. At a few minutes' notice they can mobilize the country for battle, and stand ready to do so at all times.

There have been at least four major wars between Israel and her Arab neighbors in the years since Israeli occupation took place.

Now the threat is much greater than ever, for some of the Arab states have acquired nuclear power to be used against Israel in the next great war.

Israel has nuclear power as well, and would not

fail to use it in a preemptive strike if she knew the forces of the Arab and Soviet world would soon be used against her.

When you consider the forces against Israel, it is hard to believe, apart from the power of God to protect her, how she has lasted so long.

Israel has 138,000 highly trained and skilled men in the standing Israeli Defense League. They are ready and armed at all times in the streets of Israel.

Israel has far fewer tanks, men, and arms than her Arab neighbors, but she has a will to live and a nuclear capability that could and would be used immediately if a first-strike position could save her. She has everything to lose when she loses.

EGYPT IS NOT LISTED AS AN ADVERSARY TO ISRAEL IN THIS OIL WAR.

Strange as it may seem, Ezekiel jumped right over Egypt in disclosing that Ethiopia and Libya would fight with the Arab league against Israel.

Egypt and Israel under Israeli Prime Minister Begin and the late Egyptian President Sadat have signed peace treaties and opened up the Suez Canal to Israeli shipping, and are now exchanging ambassadors and opening embassies.

Cultural exchanges will take place, and for once Egypt's large armies will not fight against Israel, according to the prophecy of Ezekiel.

With Egypt being out of the military lineup, it forces the other Arab nations, especially the PLO, to bring the Soviets into the fray, thus fitting perfectly into Biblical prophecy.

In the Ezekiel account, Magog attacks Israel after Israel has been brought back by the sword "in the latter years." This battle could not have been fought before A.D. 70 (and never was). Therefore this is the perfect timing for Ezekiel's Middle East war.

Ezekiel states that Magog (Russia) comes to take a spoil. When you leave off the first two letters you have the word oil, which Russia wants and must have. To top off their desire to get the oil for themselves is the possibility of forcing the United States to its knees in capitulation to the Soviet forces without even a war.

Peaceful cooperation and surrender would suit the Soviets much better than an all-out confrontation with the United States.

But this will never happen.

The Soviets may try, but they will not win this war. Prophecy clearly indicates that God will raise up a sword against Magog:

> And I will call for a sword against him throughout all my mountains, saith the Lord God: every man's sword shall be against his brother (Ezekiel 38:21).

From this prophetical text comes the inspiration to believe that Israel will have a military ally in the United States fighting by her side when the war breaks out.

It could be through the forces of NATO, for if Europe believes that by winning the war in the Middle East the Soviets would cut off their oil supply, NATO will willingly go to battle, thereby immediately involving the United States, along with Canadians and allies of the Western European forces.

The prophecy further indicates divine intervention to win this war against such formidable foes:

> *And I will plead against him with pestilence and with blood; and I will rain upon him and upon his bands and upon the many people that are with him an overflowing rain, and great hailstones, fire, and brimstone* (Ezekiel 38:22).

God moves heaven to protect Israel in spite of her unregenerate condition at that time. Thus, along with allies helping her, God comes to the rescue operation and finalizes the operation in the annihilation of Israel's enemies.

The destruction is further amplified in Ezekiel 39:

> *And I will smite thy bow out of thy left hand and will cause thine arrows to fall out of thy right hand. Thou shalt fall upon the mountains of Israel, thou and all thy bands and the people that is with thee. I will give thee unto the ravenous birds of every sort, and to the beasts of the field, to be devoured. Thou shalt fall upon the open field; for I have spoken it,*

saith the Lord. And I will send a fire on Magog, and among them that dwell carelessly in the isles; and they shall know that I am the Lord. (Ezekiel 39:3-6).

The nuclear disarmament of the Soviet Union takes place in Israel and in Russia itself, according to the best interpretations of this prophecy.

Double judgment falls, first in Israel and the nations of the Middle East (where this terrible war is waged) and then by God reaching up and destroying Magog, the lands and leaders of the Soviet Union.

God, knowing full well that the ones who planned the war are not in the actual war, reaches up and crushes them simultaneously with their military defeat in the hills of Israel.

Could this "fire on Magog" be European and American nuclear power destroying the Soviet Union? Certainly it could.

God uses earthly as well as heavenly powers to do His will. It could very well be the nuclear powers of the United States involved in this destruction.

This provokes the question, in light of all the nuclear warheads aimed at the United States and its allies, of what happens to Europe, the United States, and Canada in all of this.

Could we be destroyed?

Will Israel be destroyed?

Will the Arabs be wiped out completely?

Will all the Soviet people be destroyed?

Could Europe be wiped off the face of the map?

I believe the answer is no to all the above questions, for the following reasons.

Israel will not be destroyed, for God said they would dwell safely. There will be bloodshed, death, and annihilation of many Israelis, but the nation itself will not be destroyed, nor the majority of the people.

They will then know who God is and will have a national revival on their hands, as indicated earlier in this book. This is no doubt the point at which 144,000 Jews turn to Christ overnight.

The Arab nations will not be totally destroyed. Perhaps the nations themselves will barely be touched but the armies will be destroyed and possibly their leaders as well (who unquestioningly will be involved in the battle itself).

The Arab nations will be preserved because they have a mighty revival coming their way as the Messiah takes the throne after the Battle of Armageddon. According to Isaiah 19, this will happen when Egypt, the other Arab nations, and Israel are one with the Lord.

Europe will be bleeding badly all over. If there is a war involving both Eastern and Western Europe, then it is only reasonable to assume that both sides will suffer terribly.

Eastern Europe, including the Soviet Union, will be wiped out as Magog has a "destruction of fire descend upon it."

If there is an exchange of nuclear power from

the East to the West and vice versa, destruction of many cities in Europe could happen in the aftermath of missiles being launched by the Soviets against Paris, London, Rome, Brussels, etc.

North America could be hurt badly as well, though not totally destroyed.

Several U.S. generals state that the majority of the U.S. would be wiped out. I do not believe this for several reasons.

First, God said, "Whoever blesses Israel shall be blessed, and whoever curses Israel shall be cursed."

America and Canada have helped Israel tremendously. The United States has been behind virtually every move which the Israelis have desired to make, with some exceptions of West Bank settlements.

The United States and Canada have afforded millions of Jews a home and a place to rise to the highest of positions in power, politics, and money.

They are in every industry and lead the nation in many areas, including the entertainment industry of Beverly Hills and Hollywood.

Every communications medium has on its corporate board some American Jews. They abound in the medical world of North America, as well as in education, government, and you name it!

God has to keep His Word. We have been a friend to the Jew, whether we were right on other issues or not!

Secondly, it would be difficult for me to believe

that God would allow the godless regimes of Communistic butchers to kill the American dream, inasmuch as North America has done more to "preach the gospel to every creature" and keep the Great Commission of Jesus Christ than any other area of the world (and of all of them combined).

Consider all the medical missions, hospitals, and institutions that have been built. Consider all the schools, colleges, and leper colonies that have been established. Then add the churches of the world and of North America, plus the Christian broadcasting in radio and television, plus the printed pages produced, and you have the greatest area of the whole world for the promotion and production of the gospel of Christianity.

Would God allow a godless, Christless, Communistic power guilty of inhuman butcher to conquer and destroy the last bastion of Christianity? No.

Thirdly, North Americans (in cooperation with the Judeo-Christian heritage of compassion for others) have done more to alleviate world suffering through actual aid to millions of people than any other nation or group of nations on earth.

Great Britain colonized and taught a form of Christianity as she went, establishing missions, etc., but nothing like the powers of North America in virtually every country of the world.

When there were wars, the Americans fought on the side of freedom for all involved.

When they needed food, they got ours. When earthquakes shook the nations and destroyed cities and population centers, it was American aid that reached them.

Floods, famine, and calamities came, and the Americans were there helping, giving, and rebuilding months after the ravages came.

From the Cambodian refugees to the Cuban thousands, it is still the American compassion emanating from our religious heritage that takes over while most other nations turn them away.

We have not lost everything yet. There are millions of Americans who still feel the same about life, love, and the well-being of others.

There are still leaders in this country and Canada who very much care about what happens to the rest of the starving world.

North Americans have fulfilled the Great Commission better than any other group of people in the world.

North Americans have fulfilled the Sermon on the Mount more efficiently than any other nation or group of nations.

North America has never kicked the Jew into the sea and passed legislation making it impossible for him to live among us, as has England, France, Germany, etc. in days gone by.

Egypt cursed the Jew. The Assyrians of the past cursed the Jews. The Greeks, Romans, Babylonians, Medes, Persians, Greeks, Turks, and Nazis all mistreated the Jews, and where are these people today?

Either they are vanished from the face of the earth or are in captivity to dictators or are second-rate nations hardly visible today on the political scene at all. They have become receiving nations—poor and neglected, with terrible leadership.

God kept His Word in judgment, and He is also keeping His Word with respect to the blessings He mentioned (Genesis 12:2,3).

In blessing Israel we bring blessing on this nation and its people for generation after generation. This has been true since America's inception.

Not only did God want to build America because He would use it in prophetical fulfillments, but also because He wanted it to be a home for the wandering Jew. This has been Israel's bank; this is where most of the money supporting Israel for over 30 years has come from.

Jews making great money supported the cause of Israel. Gentiles, in government and out, passed on monetary benefits to Israel never heard of before from one nation to another.

Would God allow a completely godless regime to destroy a nation that had done these three things so well?

I firmly believe that this would be against God's Word and thus against God's will for this nation.

WOULD GOD ALLOW THIS NATION TO SUFFER FROM NUCLEAR WAR?

Yes, that could happen. We deserve some judgment for the sins of our nation.

We have not always been right in national trends and government legislation.

We have allowed the rights of the gay movement. The Bible is firmly against homosexuality and clearly states God's position in Romans chapter 1.

We are permitting legalized abortion, the wholesale killing of the unborn, which is clearly against God's plan.

We appease the Communists rather than oppose them forthrightly. We sell them sophisticated equipment and much-needed food, and by so doing we allow them to keep slaves in labor camps throughout the Soviet Union.

We could be bombed or be the recipients of their powerful intercontinental ballistic missiles, which are already aimed at this country.

We could have *some* devastation without being completely destroyed, but just set back sufficiently to let Europe rise as the world government it is prophetically destined to become under the Antichrist.

It is possible that with or without an economic depression, this method could be employed by our Lord to reduce this nation to a second-class position and simultaneously allow Europe to rise to world prominence.

Either we will have a cataclysmic economic depression or we will be affected by Soviet nuclear power.

I prefer the former to the latter.

I believe personally that it will be the former rather than the latter. It is difficult to believe that God would allow the Communists to even hurt this Christian country.

But God could allow us to suffer internally through an economic depression while Western Europe rises.

THE WAR WITH THE SOVIET UNION AND THE ARABS AGAINST ISRAEL WILL BE AT LEAST SEVEN YEARS BEFORE THE COMING OF CHRIST AND THE BEGINNING OF THE MILLENNIAL REIGN OF CHRIST IN JERUSALEM.

The reason for the foregoing statement is because of interesting verses in Ezekiel 39:9,10 which reveal the Israelis using the weapons of war for seven years afterward.

> *They that dwell in the cities of Israel shall go forth, and shall set on fire and burn the weapons, both the shields and the bucklers, the bows and the arrows, and the handstaves and the spears, and they shall burn them with fire seven years, so that they shall take no wood out of the field, neither cut down any out of the forests; for they shall burn the weapons with fire; and they shall spoil those that spoiled them, and rob those that robbed them, saith the Lord God* (Ezekiel 39:9,10).

This is a direct reference to the conservative Israelis doing what they have done after every war and skirmish with the Arabs. They have used their enemies' tanks, guns, weapons, and armor over and over again on their own side, after refinishing them to suit their own needs and style of warfare.

I have been in the Israeli rebuilding plant outside Tel Aviv, watching the Israelis take captured Russian T-40 tanks and change them to suit their own necessities.

When the Russians built the tanks they had the ammunition stored near the top of the tank, so that any kind of a hit would worsen the situation for the men inside.

The Israelis put the ammunition storage down lower, between the tractor-like wheels, and thereby saved many lives and continue the usefulness of several thousand tanks which they confiscated from their Arab enemies (who had received them in aid from the Soviets).

This is exactly what the Israelis will do with the weapons left after the end of the great oil war.

Obviously there will be great supplies left in the fields and in areas used for hidden storage of military supplies nearby.

There will be tanks and many kinds of guns. This is possibly a reference to the nuclear-powered vehicles for land, sea, and air operation that could be left in the utter chaos of the ending of the war (as it is predicted to end).

Billions of dollars of weapons utilizing energy sources could be available to the frugal Israelis.

When we understand the barrenness of the land

from the standpoint of trees in 1948, and how many millions of trees have been planted by Israelis and tourists from the world over, and the value the Israeli government puts on the trees to stop soil erosion and produce fruit, then we understand why this verse is so important to them.

The war will no doubt bring great devastation to the foliage of the land. Israel is a breadbasket of fruits, vegetables, olive trees, etc. It is currently the greatest exporter of fruit in the world, according to the latest statistics.

To an Israeli with sloping property this is an important fact. The roots of trees hold soil to the ground, and thus what the farmer has planted will remain and not wash away in the torrential rains they have there.

This prophecy also takes into consideration the fact that Israeli industries may be badly hurt in the war. Any kind of enemy attack on an enemy's industrial might is devastating to the country.

We are speaking of modern times, with modern conveniences, energy, and engines.

This could well be a reference to the ailing Israeli industry (which will suffer terribly in the war) utilizing the nuclear power of the enemy for its own social and industrial good for seven years.

Whatever the reason and whatever the meaning, the prophecy indicates that this war with the Soviets and Arabs *will come at least seven years before the Battle of Armageddon and/or the beginn-*

ing of the millennial reign of Christ.

The reason for this is that in the Battle of Armageddon all will be destroyed, and by the time the millennial reign of Christ is set up (in the newly built City of Jerusalem, with the much-enlarged temple to be built there, described in Ezekiel chapters 40 to 48), there is a completely new land, (no longer needing Soviet nuclear power to sustain it) on into the millennial reign of Christ.

All of this must come *before* the millennial reign, and thus before the Battle of Armageddon and before Daniel's seventieth-week prophecy.

Keep in mind that all is destroyed in devastating fashion at Armageddon. There will be no factories to burn the nuclear power with or in.

In stating that they will "rob those that robbed them," the prophecy indicates that there will be great spoils from the war to the benefit of Israel.

This could very well include some of the oil of the neighboring states of the Arabs—oil that could be used by the Israelis for a time.

In Daniel's seventy-week prophecy there are seventy weeks of years covering God's special dealings with Israel (outlined by the prophet in Daniel 9:24-27).

The Antichrist makes a covenant with Israel to protect them for seven years. Again this mystical number of seven pops up with respect to this time for the Israelis.

It is possible that the Antichrist will be attacked simultaneously as the governmental head of

Europe's ten-nation entity at this time.

We know the following facts.

A. He is invited to take over Europe after they become ten nations together.

B. He takes over as invited, and works to produce unity and harmony among the ten nations that act as clay and iron with one another.

C. This could take a little longer than most of us fully realize or anticipate, in our hurry to make prophecy fulfill itself. It could take several years before he has full control of the ten nations and has fully blended them together. While he is working with them as their leader, and at the same time working with the false church in order to gain European recognition and world power, he is attacked by the Soviets as they attack in the Middle East also.

He is saved by the power of God being poured out upon the enemy in Magog and in the hills and mountains of Israel.

He will have been involved in the war through NATO, then attacked viciously and suddenly, as predicted in Daniel 11:40:

> *And at the time of the end shall the king of the south push at him; and the king of the north shall come against him like a whirlwind, with chariots and with horsemen and*

with many ships; and he shall enter into the countries, and shall overflow and pass over.

The Antichrist is attacked as Israel is attacked, but note that the Antichrist is not in Israel at the time of the attack! He is elsewhere ... Where? Presiding over the ten nations by whom he has been given authority. He is in Europe.

The "King of the South" is a reference to Moslem black and Arab states from Africa coming against him, who are also Communist states following Magog.

The King of the North is the Soviet Union, which leads the attack on perhaps three fronts—Europe, Africa, and Israel, via the Middle East nations.

It is only after this attack by the King of the North that later (and we do not know how much later) the Antichrist marches on Israel and takes over Jerusalem and the temple.

It does stand to reason that he will remain in his own Western European capitol and let the dead bury the dead in Israel right after the war.

Why go to the area so recently devastated? If the oil wells and supplies of the Middle East have been destroyed, then there will be an important time of rebuilding this energy source.

The Middle East will be recovering from the greatest war in anyone's history. The bloodbath will be unprecedented and the destruction of industry everywhere will be overwhelming and will take much time, money, and skill to rebuild.

In the aftermath of this war and suffering and

devastation, great help and aid comes to Israel from this Man of Sin and his allies.

> *And he shall confirm the covenant with many for one week; and in the midst of the week he shall cause the sacrifice and the oblation to cease, and for the overspreading of abominations he shall make it desolate, even until the consummation, and that determined shall be poured upon the desolate* (Daniel 9:27).

The Antichrist makes a covenant and comes in peaceably, as indicated in a further revelation by Daniel.

> *But he shall come in peaceably and obtain the kingdom by flatteries. And with the arms of a flood shall they be overflown from before him, and shall be broken; yea, also the prince of the covenant. . . . He shall enter peaceably even upon the fattest places of the province* (Daniel 11:21-24).

He is a man of deceit and guile. He is energized by Satan and fools the nations of the earth for a time.

We who are students of the amazing prophecies of the Bible have a tendency to push prophecies together and try to rush their final fulfillment, without giving proper time for all things to be properly ready.

When the fullness of time comes, all will fit together perfectly.

5

Shockwaves from the Kingdom of the Antichrist

The Antichrist comprises one of the most intriguing and mystifying of all the prophecies of the Bible.

Daniel predicted him first, before any other prophet, disciple, or Biblical writer.

The Book of Daniel, by the way, is the most attacked book of the Bible, along with Genesis and Revelation.

Genesis is attacked because it is the complete story of creation and God's dealing with man and his original sin. People do not like our beginning, our sinning, and God's dealings with us. So Genesis and its credibility stand attacked daily. Some churches have even denounced the first ten chapters of Genesis as some style of fairy story.

But if you do away with Genesis, then you do away with man's fall into sin. If man has not fallen from his original state and was not divinely created by an Almighty God, then you can have evolution, with no need for a real Savior, for there is no longer any sin question to deal with.

These religious organizations and educational institutions can then do whatever they wish with Jesus Christ: He was profound, a great philosopher, a marvelous teacher, and the epitome of wisdom, but certainly not a Savior, for we don't need one.

They attack Revelation because it is the story of the end of it all. Everything man has created, achieved, and accomplished in science, religion, education, and sin, will all come to one great end.

Many people reject the Biblical account of the end of it all, even as they do the beginning of it all, and attack both the first and last books of the Bible.

But the book attacked the most is Daniel. Why is this so?

Daniel was the most detailed prophet. He forthrightly plunged into the many dens of lions he faced and came out on top by the grace of Almighty God until his days were ended. Daniel was so profoundly in tune with God about the future and was so right and precise that he is still the most attacked prophet of the Bible.

And yet Daniel probably never saw the church age that we are living in now. Daniel did not see the Gentiles being grafted into the divine olive tree (Romans chapters 9-11).

Daniel did not see the 2000 years of the church age, the Gentile Christians, the coming of the Holy Spirit, or the falling away of the Jew from God's direct dealing with them.

But what He did see astounds us to this day.

He saw the end of the Babylonian Empire, the empire of the mighty Medes and Persians, the empire of the Greco-Macedonians under Alexander the Great, and the Roman Empire. Then, remarkably, he saw into our day and predicted that then nations would rise out of the old Roman Empire and form a world government.

Daniel in the midst of these prophecies was allowed to catch a glimpse of the coming Messiah.

God revealed this phenomenal prophecy to Him only once, and he wrote about it clearly, perhaps not understanding all that He wrote about.

It is worthy of our comment here as we go into Daniel's teaching of the Antichrist.

He stated, "Messiah shall be cut off, but not for himself" (Daniel 9:26).

Daniel had been blessed of God with a revelation that the Lord had allowed him to receive concerning seventy weeks of years predicted about Israel and God's dealings with them as a nation.

Daniel had been reading from Jeremiah's prophecy about Israel (chapter 29) and was puzzled by Jeremiah speaking of God dealing with Israel for the seventy weeks of years.

He prayed and the Lord dispatched the angel Gabriel to communicate the interpretation to Daniel as follows:

> And he informed me and talked with me, and said, O Daniel, I am now come forth to give thee skill and understanding. At the begin-

> ning of thy supplications this commandment
> came forth, and I am come to show thee, for
> thou art greatly beloved; therefore under-
> stand the matter, and consider the vision.
> Seventy weeks are determined upon thy peo-
> ple (seventy weeks of years means 490 years,
> as each day is a year) and upon thy holy city,
> to finish the transgression, and to make an
> end of sins, and to make reconciliation for ini-
> quity, and to bring in everlasting
> righteousness, and to seal up the vision and
> prophecy, and to anoint the Most Holy (Daniel
> 9:22-24).

Notice the importance of this vision and its interpretation to those in heaven and on earth. God was
sending an angel to tell a prophet on earth what
was going to happen to Israel, and it turned out to
be one of the most important messages of all to
Israel in the Book of Daniel, apart from what
Zechariah predicted about the return of the Lord
Himself.

Daniel was told that the message in Jeremiah's
text meant that God was to have 490 years of
special dealings with the house of Israel.

During this 490-year period certain things were
going to happen, some of which were revealed to
Daniel in the following verses and some of which
were not.

But the first point is that during this 490-year
period all things would bring about the anointing
of the Most Holy.

That meant to Daniel the coming of the Messiah, long awaited by the Jewish people as their Deliverer.

God further revealed the profoundness of this prophecy to Daniel by telling him that by the time this 490-year period ended, there would be an end of sins, reconciliation for iniquity, and the ushering in of everlasting righteousness.

This was so remarkable that Daniel could hardly contain himself with such revelations.

This meant that the kingdom age would be on earth when these things were done during the period of 490 years.

Only English-version Bibles have trouble with the seventy weeks of years adding up to 490 years in total.

In any Jewish Bible it is clearly written 490 years, or seventy weeks of years, with each day being a year. (Seventy weeks times seven days equals 490 years.)

The term "weeks of years" was not new to Daniel or to the Jews. Jacob the son of Isaac was courting his wife-to-be, Rachel, in Genesis chapter 29. His father-in-law tricked him into marrying Leah, the eldest daughter, first. Then Laban told him he could have Rachel for his wife if he would work another "week" for her. He had already worked a "week" for her, but got Leah instead. The Bible clearly states, as an indication to us, that Jacob worked another *seven years* for Rachel, and that he married her too after he had fulfilled her *week of years*.

The period in Daniel was seventy weeks of years determined upon the Holy City and the holy people. It was a marvelous message of prophecy for Daniel, who was in Babylonian captivity at the time (which was to last seventy years), but the greater interpretation involved seventy weeks of years, and this was what God was trying to teach Daniel.

Daniel understood that God was teaching him about 490 years of dealings with Israel, and at the end of this time would come the Messiah, everlasting righteousness, and the end of sins of Israel. He knew that this was the long-awaited time predicted by others, and the time that all Israel looked for.

Then God through the angel Gabriel told Daniel when the time would begin and when it would end, but without giving him all the details.

> *Know therefore and understand that from the going forth of the commandment to restore and to build Jerusalem unto Messiah the Prince shall be seven weeks, and sixty-two weeks* (Daniel 9:25).

Daniel had just had revealed to him when the Messiah was coming in terms of years! It must have stunned and thrilled him to have the Lord reveal such a wonderful revelation to him!

Daniel knew that seven weeks was 49 years in terms of actual time, and then a pause was to come, for the angel Gabriel went on to say nothing about what would happen in 49 years, but added 62 *more* weeks of years to the seven, making a total of 69 weeks of years, or 483 years in all.

The 49 years would be followed by 434 years, together making 483 years. This left one week of years to be fulfilled, and after that the Messiah would come.

Nehemiah chapter 2 records the actual "going forth of the commandment to restore and build Jerusalem" by King Artaxerxes to Nehemiah.

Gabriel said it would be a period of 49 years and then 434 years until the Messiah would appear. And 49 years after King Artaxerxes gave the commandment to Nehemiah to go to Jerusalem was the end of the Old Testament prophecy of Malachi!

The Old Testament was done and the vision of those books completed. The angel gave knowledge of something happening at the end of 49 years, but did not say exactly what. He only paused and went on.

Then came the 400 silent years between the prophecy of Malachi and the beginning of the New Testament writings.

Christ was born, then later died in Jerusalem. He was "cut off, but not for Himself" in year 34 of His life on earth, thus marvelously fulfilling the 434 years of the prophecy. Joining that with the 49 years to complete the Old Testament, we have a total of 483 years of time during which God dealt specifically with Israel.

Jesus predicted the ruination of the temple and

the dispersion of the Jews to the four quarters of the earth in Luke 21:5,6,24 and Matthew 24:2 (with reference to the destruction of the second temple in Jerusalem).

Paul refers in Romans chapters 9-11 to the cutting off of the Jews from the olive-tree relationship they had with God.

Frequently, as we noted earlier, Paul alludes to the well-known fact that they had been cut off and that the wild olive branch of the Gentiles had been grafted in instead, but that the Jews would come back to be grafted in later on, after the times of the Gentiles are fulfilled.

"Christ came to His own, and His own received Him not." *This marked the beginning of a time when God would stop dealing with Israel nationally.* He would continue His dealings with some of them individually, but not nationally.

God's dealings with Israel as a nation would begin again only after they came back *as a nation.*

God's clock stopped ticking for the Jew 2000 years ago. Thereafter Jerusalem was burned and the temple destroyed.

There would be a long pause in the course of God's dealings with Israel. God would not cast them off forever, as Paul wrote, but they would be punished for not accepting His only Son, their Savior Jesus Christ (John 1:11).

Ezekiel predicted that a great temple was going to be built and occupied by the Lord (in chapters 40 to 48 of his revelation). But that before that time the Jew would be dispersed, return home, be persecuted, go to war with Magog and Arab states, and have this great oil war that we have been speaking of.

When we read Ezekiel chapters 36 and 37 we learn that God promised to bring them all home to the land of their father Abraham. After they were there, Magog would attack and be destroyed.

While Israel was dispersed around the world, God stopped dealing with them as a nation. The fulfillment of this national prophecy was stopped. God's clock stopped ticking for the nation as long as the nation was not intact and Jerusalem was not theirs.

Jews have been in virtually every nation under the sun for the two thousand years of the dispersion (*diaspora,* as they call it).

They came back to the land due to may circumstances, including the Nazi torture and Holocaust, which drove them to their own home at last.

Then they needed time to organize themselves, build the barren land, plant their crops, and give birth to a new generation of Israeli babies. They needed to let some time pass so those babies could grow up and become a natural-born generation of Jews occupying the land of Palestine again as *Sabras*—those born in Israel.

> *And Jesus spoke to them a parable: Behold the fig tree, and all the trees. When they shoot forth, ye see and know that summer is*

> *now near at hand. So likewise ye, when ye see*
> *these things come to pass, know that the*
> *Kingdom of God is near at hand. Verily I say*
> *unto you, This generation shall not pass*
> *away till all be fulfilled* (Luke 21:29-32).

The fig tree refers to the national restoration of the house of Israel. Politically they will be restored before they are grafted in again to God spiritually.

The olive-tree prophecies refer to the spiritual rehabilitation and restoration of Israel as a nation (Romans chapter 11).

We have seen the fig tree blossom. The olive tree will come during the Tribulation period, but especially when Christ reveals Himself to the Jews at His second coming to the Mount of Olives.

Daniel predicted that there would be seventy weeks of years of God's dealings with Israel specifically.

Daniel 9:26 speaks of the death of the Messiah being 483 years after King Artaxerxes gave the commandment to Nehemiah to rebuild the city. And Jesus Christ died on the cross just after year 483 spoken of by Gabriel. That is a marvelous prophecy to use with your Jewish nonbelieving friends and acquaintances to win them to Christ. I have had many occasions to use it while dealing with Israelis and American Jews.

But notice that Daniel said that the Messiah would be cut off—die—*after* week 69. Christ would not die as the Messiah *during* the 69 weeks, but *afterward*.

Also, there would come a prince (not capitalized) who would destroy the city and the sanctuary and would bring desolations.

This too would be after week 69 but before the beginning again of God's clock and dealings with the nation of Israel.

The reason for God stopping His dealings with Israel nationally is because of their rejection of Christ on earth during His ministry as He came to them and they "received him not" (John 1:11).

Christ died *after* week 69 had ended and Jerusalem was sacked and the temple destroyed.

The seventieth week of years, which would start God's clock ticking again for the Jews as a nation, would begin again *after* Israel came back home, *after* the Holocaust, *after* the Antichrist takes the reins of government in Europe in his own hands, *after* they elect the Man of Sin to power, and perhaps *after* the war with Magog.

This will do one great thing not done yet to date—cause the uniting of the city of Jerusalem under Jewish rule completely and the rebuilding of the temple. Arabs still live there, govern in part there, and worship there (and in other parts of the land under Israeli jurisdiction).

The Arabs have their temple there—the Dome of the Rock Mosque and the other silver-domed Mosque yards away—where they pray to Allah five times every day, thereby desecrating the area of the original temple site (where also the second temple was, that Jesus ministered and taught in).

There is something special to the Lord about that temple site with respect to the fulfillment of prophecy.

It appears that as long as the temple is not built (which was always of singular importance to the prophets of the Old Testament in the latter years) *the prophetic clock may not tick yet.*

Is it possible that, as a result of this forthcoming war with Magog and the others, the Dome of the Rock Mosque will be destroyed and Jews will be able to rebuild their own temple? Certainly it is not only possible but most probable.

It would take an act of war to destroy it, as the Israelis would never take it upon themselves to destroy another man's house of worship.

Both earthquakes and wars are predicted for Jerusalem. These will undoubtedly destroy the Mosque!

The Jews will renovate the land and rebuild the temple (which will be the third Jewish temple in history and will be occupied by the Antichrist).

As soon as the war is over with Russia, and the Arabs are defeated and the Mosque is destroyed, the temple will be built.

At that point God starts the clock ticking with national Israel again. (It is also the time when the Antichrist makes his seven-year covenant with Israel.)

The clock probably begins to tick *after* the temple is built, during which time the Antichrist is in Europe still rebuilding after the Russian war.

Much aid flows to Israel from the U.S. and other areas of the world. She rebuilds after burying the dead as indicated earlier.

The first thing that happens to unify Israel and bring them back to a God-consciousness after feeling God's mighty power during the war is the rebuilding of the temple.

It could go on while others are burying dead Arabs, Russians, Eastern Europeans, and Africans in the mountains of Israel during that seven-year period (Ezekiel 39:7-11).

There could be a time of regrouping of forces for the Antichrist in Europe after the destruction brought on by the war before he enacts legislation against or for Israel. His first acts for Israel will be the signing of a covenant of protection, including trade agreements with the Common Market offering Israel unusual trade benefits with the European allies that now stand behind her.

He wants friendship with Israel, and he comes peaceably to her with aid.

At this time the temple will already be built or is being built. Israel will go through a partial national cleansing of soul and mind, and though not ready to be a Christian nation yet, will realize that the God of Abraham is alive and did reveal Himself to them in the miraculous deliverance of Israel from their terrible foes in that war to end all wars.

They will have seen God in action. He said:

> *Thus will I magnify myself and sanctify myself, and I will be known in the eyes of*

> *many nations, and they shall know that I am the Lord* (Ezekiel 38:23).

> *So will I make my holy name known in the midst of my people Israel; and I will not let them pollute my holy name anymore; and the heathen shall know that I am the Lord, the Holy One in Israel* (Ezekiel 39:7).

These two verses indicate that both the world and Israel will recognize God's presence, power, and reality.

In Revelation chapter 7, after the horses' ride of the Apocalypse of chapter 6, we have the 144,000 Jews accepting Christ. But simultaneous with this religious move in Israel will be the building of the temple as a resurrection of the faith of Israel in God Himself, and a revival of the nations.

> *After this I beheld, and lo, a great multitude, which no man could number, of all nations and kindreds and people and tongues, stood before the throne, and before the Lamb, clothed with white robes, and palms in their hands, and cried with a loud voice, saying, Salvation to our God, who sitteth upon the throne, and unto the Lamb. . . . And one of the elders answered, saying unto me, What are these which are arrayed in white robes, and whence came they? And I said unto him, Sir, thou knowest. And he said to me, These are they which came out of great tribulation, and have washed their robes and made them*

white in the blood of the Lamb. (Revelation 7:9-14).

It is clearly a group from every nation who are in heaven at this time (which is after the war) who have found Christ as their personal Savior and are rejoicing in the other world.

Were they saved during the terrible period of the war, and just afterward, as God revealed Himself to the nations? Quite possibly.

Daniel reveals the covenant to be made the the Jews for a period of one week. This is one week of years, or seven years, thereby completing the vision of Jeremiah and the vision of Daniel about the seventy weeks of years.

The clock will then be ticking again. God will once again be dealing with Israel as a nation.

The fullness of the Gentiles will have come in! The city will have been reunited under Israeli control. The temple will have been built. The Antichrist will be helping in any way possible, and by false peace will be destroying many people as he builds their confidence in himself, only to turn against them shortly.

But remember that there could be a period of time to rebuild the land and the temple after the war with Russia, before the seven-year covenant with Israel is signed by the leader in Europe.

How much time could elapse is unknown, but it is reasonable to assume a few years anyway. It could be anywhere from three to five years or longer. The wheels of government grind slowly.

Where will the Antichrist come from? Will he be resurrected from the dead? Is he an Israeli? A European? An Arab?

For the best answers to the above questions that so many people ask about the coming Man of Sin, it is best that we consider first his names and then a description of his personality, character, and life's plan.

He is called by the following names in the Bible.

1. Eleventh horn (Daniel 7:20)
2. King of fierce countenance (Daniel 8:23)
3. Prince (Daniel 9:26,27)
4. False christ (Matthew 24:24)
5. Antichrist (1 John 2:18,22)
6. Beast (Revelation 13:1-3)
7. Man of sin (2 Thessalonians 2:1-8)

It has been said by many Bible expositors that the Antichrist will be a resurrected evil personage of the past, based on an interpretation of Revelation 17:8 which says this about the Antichrist as a beast:

> *The beast that thou sawest was, and is not, and shall ascend out of the bottomless pit, and go into perdition* (Revelation 17:8).

It is entirely possible that he will be a resurrected personality of the past who is clothed in a new body of the present, perfectly preserved by the power of God until this revelation of him.

Adding fuel to this interpretation is an additional

verse in Revelation 13 that seems to add weight to the argument:

> And I saw one of his heads as it were wounded to death; and his deadly wound was healed; and all the world wondered after the beast (Revelation 13:3).

Taking both verses together, one can easily understand the theory that he will be a resurrected personality out of the distant past.

Theories have run from him being Judas Iscariot, Nimrod of the tower of Babel, Antiochus Epiphanes (of the 400 silent years, who persecuted Jews and offered a female swine on a Jewish altar), down to John F. Kennedy and others.

I personally lean in the direction that the Antichrist, Mr. 666 as I call him now, could well be a resurrected personality out of the past, perfectly preserved by God for such an hour as this.

Daniel chapter 8 sheds much light on the doctrine of the Antichrist for those of us concerned deeply about this Bible truth.

Here we have the vision given to Daniel of a ram and goat fighting. The ram was the empire of the Medes and Persians, about to be destroyed by the goat (the Greeks under Alexander the Great), who was represented in this vision by a great horn between his eyes.

The goat rammed the ram and killed it, but the horn broke on the goat. Alexander the Great died shortly after taking over the known world, and wept because there were no more worlds to conquer.

The prophecy goes on to teach us in verses 8-27 that when the horn broke, four others would take its place in power. So, when Alexander died, the four leading generals of Greece, located in various areas with their respective armies of Greece, took over the Greek Empire.

Here is the key to the original source of the Antichrist.

> And out of one of them [horns] came forth a little horn, which waxed exceeding great, toward the south, toward the east, and toward the pleasant land. And it waxed great. . . . And in the latter time of their kingdom . . . a king of fierce countenance and understanding an evil philosophy shall stand up. And his power shall be mighty . . . and he shall destroy . . . and prosper . . . and shall destroy the might and holy people. . . . He shall also stand up against the Prince of princes [Christ], but he shall be broken (Daniel 8:9,10,23-25).

When Alexander the Great died, the four generals were in Greece, Turkey, Egypt, and Syria. "Out of one of these" shall the Antichrist come. He is alive now, today, waiting for his moment of glory to come. The Antichrist could come out one of these nations.

A resurrected personality out of the past (Revelation 17:8) could even mean a resurrected spirit out of Alexander the Great, placed into the human body of a current rejecter of divine truth. God could use the body and soul of a reprobate to house the spirit of the preborn Antichrist. Only time will tell.

That he will claim to be the Messiah will be the "strong delusion that God will send," the "lie" that those who reject Christ will want to believe and by doing so will be condemned (2 Thessalonians 2:1-12).

The beast is described as having seven heads and ten horns:

> And I [John] stood upon the sand of the sea, and saw a beast rise up out of the sea, having seven heads and ten horns, and upon his horns ten crowns, and upon his heads the name of blasphemy (Revelation 13:1).

In order to understand what the seven heads really mean, it is best to let the Scriptures tell their own story and make their own interpretation.

> Here is the mind which hath wisdom. The seven heads are seven mountains on which the woman sitteth. And there are seven kings: five are fallen, and one is, and the other is not yet come; and when he cometh, he must continue a short space. And the beast that was and is not, even he is the eighth, and is of the seven, and goeth into perdition (Revelation 17:9-11).

It took me months and even years of study to fully understand this puzzle of prophecy. But when the interpretation came I rejoiced indeed.

"The seven heads are seven mountains." A mountain in the Old Testament is frequently referred to as a world government—in this case, a government that had conquered Israel and had direct dealings with Israel.

The following references can be checked for further verification of this fact.

> *Behold, I am against thee, O destroying mountain, saith the Lord, which destroyest all the earth* (Jeremiah 51:25).

God was talking to and about Babylon! and it was not a literal mountain at all. God was pronouncing doom against Babylon and called her a destroying mountain, a destroying government.

> *Son of man, set thy face toward the mountains of Israel, and prophecy against them* (Ezekiel 6:1).

God does not speak to mountains; He speaks to men and governments.

> *Also, thou son of man, prophecy unto the mountains of Israel, and say, Ye mountains of Israel, hear the word of the Lord* (Ezekiel 36:1).

This was an expression referring to a nation or a government, which the next verses in Revelation 17 will bear out.

> *The seven heads are seven mountains on which the woman sitteth* (Revelation 17:9).

The false church, the one that rejects the truth of the real God, does not sit on hills or mountains, but sits on and rules through governments and nations. It makes much more sense to interpret it this way.

If this is true, and the seven heads are seven world governments, then the next statement makes sense too: "And there are seven kings." There you have it—seven kings that are over the seven governments or nations that God is speaking of.

In addition, the verses say, "Five are fallen and one is." Five literal hills or mountains don't fall or get Scriptural recognition as having kings. But five world governments had conquered Israel and later disappeared. Egypt, Assyria, Babylon (Chaldeans), Medes and Persians, Greeks had all come and gone.

Now, at the time of the writing of this prophecy, "One is"—Rome was in power. Next comes a statement bewildering many people.

> *The other is not yet come, and when he cometh he must continue a short space* (Revelation 17:10).

This one really upset me, because for a long time I thought the reference to "he and him" was to the Antichrist. But it is not. It is a reference to the next world government, referred to in the masculine gender as government number seven.

The Antichrist comes as government number eight! The next verse states his rise:

The beast that was and is not, even he is the eighth, and is of the seven, and goeth into perdition (Revelation 17:11).

The Antichrist is the eighth world government, but was of the other seven. What does this mean? Simply that he is the essence of evil of all world governments of the past. He is the sum total of evil to the superlative degree. He is energized by Satan and is the greatest tool of the Devil that God ever allows turned loose on earth.

The Antichrist is the eighth world government after the death of the seventh world government, which has not been named in the verses as yet.

Five are fallen, and one is, and the other is not yet come; and when he cometh, he must continue a short space (Revelation 17:10).

We know who the first five were, and we now know who number six was. We also know who number eight will be. It will be the government of the beast, the Antichrist. Who and what is government number seven?

The seventh world government is about to dawn on the human race. Verse 12 of Revelation 17 fully explains the mystery of who or what is government seven, plus the second mystery: What are the ten horns that are beside the seven heads on the beast?

The ten horns which thou sawest are ten kings, which have received no kingdom as yet, but receive power as kings one hour with the beast (Revelation 17:12).

The ten horns are ten nations that have received no world power as yet, but they will receive world government, power, and recognition with the Antichrist.

We know that the ten horns are the ten nations referred to as the Common Market nations.

They are not a world power as yet, but they will receive world government status when they select their new world leader, the Antichrist. He will enable them to pull together and become great in a united form.

These nations have existed for some time independent of one another and fighting one another, but now, after their own futile try at uniting, they elect a leader who does the job because of his power, personality, and world-recognized ability. He makes them great!

They become, with his help, government number seven. Then, after making them great, he turns on them and the other nations, and makes himself government number eight.

He retains this title and enacts the powers of a world government and dictator for only 42 months, according to Revelation 13:5.

There was given unto him a mouth speaking great things and blasphemies, and power was given unto him to continue forty-two months.

Government number seven occupies world leadership for only 3½ years.

> *When he cometh, he must continue a short space* (Revelation 17:10).

This means that once the Common Market nations have Greece properly situated in position, fulfilling the prophecy, they will soon elect their world leader.

Soon after his placement, they rise to world prominence and have direct dealings with Israel as a government. The reason for this last statement is that every government named had something to do with Israel in a negative way.

Most of the political prophecies of the Bible (if not all) deal directly or indirectly with Israel. This is God dealing with Israel in many of these chapters, and thus it is governments that exercise authority over Israel that are primarily referred to.

Every government listed in the original six hurt Israel in one way or another. Following the pattern, so will governments number seven and eight.

How Europe will hurt Israel is not revealed completely except as they might assist the Antichrist in taking jurisdiction over Israel halfway through the seven-year covenant he makes with the tiny state in the Middle East.

A lot of information comes to the world of Christendom and others who are interested in the fulfillment of the amazing prophecies of the Bible.

Much of this information I have written on in books dealing with political economics and conspiracy theories that will aid in the bringing about of the one-world government leadership of Europe.

International bankers who control central banks (as the Federal Reserve System, the Bank of Canada, the Bank of England and so on) control much political power and thus influence many foreign-affairs decisions and domestic decisions in the countries where they are actively engaged in controlling the money supply and interest rates.

I will not go into this here, but I urge you to read my books entitled *How to Survive the Money Crash*, *The Coming Oil War*, and *The Greatest Banking Scandal in History*.

These are available at many bookstores in shopping malls and elsewhere, or you can write me at my address given in this book.

The spirit of Antichrist is in the world. It is in high places, for now truly:

> *We wrestle not against flesh and blood, but against principalities, against powers, against the rulers of the darkness of this world, against spiritual wickedness in high places. Wherefore take unto you the whole armor of God, that ye may be able to withstand in the evil day, and having done all, to stand* (Ephesians 6:12,13).

This is the beginning of that day!

The original Man of Sin lived in Old Testament times.

> *I saw one of his heads as it were wounded to death, and his deadly wound was healed; and all the world wondered after the beast* (Revelation 13:3).

Biblical expositors have pondered over this verse for ages. Some believe it will be a murdered and resurrected human being who will be the Antichrist, and that this murder will take place (along with his resurrection back to life) in this day in which we are now living. This would give him credibility with the nations and religions.

However, if the seven heads of the Antichrist represent the world governments that we have mentioned earlier from Egypt to this present time, all affecting Israel detrimentally, then the teaching indicates that he lived in one of the periods of those "heads" or world governments.

The terrible acts of the Antichrist (after he usurps control of Israel and the seventh world government) lead to the eighth government. HE TURNS ON ISRAEL AND REJECTS HIS OWN COVENANT WITH THEM. HE MARCHES ON ISRAEL AND JERUSALEM BECOMES HIS HOME.

> *He shall plant the tabernacles of his palace between the seas in the glorious holy mountain; yet he shall come to his end, and none shall help him* (Daniel 11:45).

He lives between the Mediterranean Sea and the

Dead Sea, and breaks his covenant with Israel to protect them.

It is very possible that the newly built temple will become his home for the 42 months that he is in Jerusalem, but if not, it will certainly house his idolatrous image.

HE TURNS ON EUROPE AND TAKES THEM OVER COMPLETELY, CREATING HIS OWN EIGHTH WORLD GOVERNMENT.

> *The ten horns out of this kingdom are ten kings that shall arise; and another shall rise after them, and he shall be diverse from the first, and he shall subdue three kings. And he shall speak great words against the Most High, and shall wear out the saints of the Most High, and think to change times and laws; and they shall be given into his hand until a time and times and the dividing of time* (Daniel 7:24,25).

Evidently when the Antichrist is through cooperating with the ten nations of the Common Market, he will readily usurp totalitarian, dictatorial control of them, but will run into opposition with three of the ten.

They will fight him, but the Bible does not say whether it will be a military battle or a political-ideological battle. It seems that it will more of the latter than the former.

> *There are seven kings: Five are fallen, and one is, and the other is not yet come; and when he*

> *cometh, he must continue a short space* (Revelation 17:10).

They only reign as a world power with him for a short time. A further rendering of prophecy teaches that it is a *very* short space of time, called "one hour."

> *The ten horns which thou sawest are ten kings, which have received no kingdom as yet, but receive power as kings one hour with the beast* (Revelation 17:12).

This is a difficult but not an indecipherable text. They receive no world dominion without the Antichrist. They struggle for it even with the help of traitors in other countries, probably even in America. (These traitors are in every free-world country.)

They fail to become world powers until they select him for their leadership over the ten nations.

Then, perhaps during or just after the time of the coming oil war with Russia in Europe and the Middle East, he completes his plans for world domination and uses them and the false church to bring about his kingdom rule.

He then becomes a world dictator.

> *And they worshipped the beast, saying, Who is like unto the beast? Who is able to make war with him?* (Revelation 13:4).

The world of his dominion will revere him, worship him, and allow him complete control over their lives.

THE ANTICHRIST THEN TAKES OVER THE TEMPLE IN JERUSALEM.

> *Let no man deceive you by any means, for that day shall not come except there come a falling away first, and that man of sin be revealed, the son of perdition, who opposeth and exalteth himself above all that is called God or that is worshipped, so that he as God sitteth in the temple of God, showing himself that he is God* (2 Thessalonians 2:3,4).

When the Antichrist takes Israel, he claims that he is their long-awaited Messiah and claims the temple as his own.

The Antichrist sets up, with the aid of the False Prophet, an image of himself in the Most Holy Place of the Jewish temple. It is called the abomination of desolation.

> *He shall confirm the covenant with many for one week [seven years]; and in the midst of the week he shall cause the sacrifice and oblation to cease, and for the overspreading of abominations he shall make it desolate, even until the consummation, and that determined shall be poured upon the desolate* (Daniel 9:27).

Again, this is a reference to his seven-year agreement with Israel and perhaps other countries in the Middle East. He uses the military, political, and economic powers of the ten nations to back up his promise of help and security.

Then, in the middle of the seven years, he breaks his covenant, marches on Israel, takes over the temple, and ends whatever worship procedure they were having there.

> *Arms shall stand on his part, and they shall pollute the sanctuary of strength, and shall take away the daily sacrifice, and they shall place the abomination that maketh desolate* (Daniel 11:31).

> *From the time that the daily sacrifice shall be taken away and the abomination that maketh desolate be set up, there shall be a thousand two hundred and ninety days* (Daniel 12:11).

This is another reference to the 42 months that the Antichrist reigns supreme in Israel and in the temple.

There is a difference in this and some prophecies that indicate he will reign 42 months or 1260 days. This says 1290 days, leaving us to speculate on the extra month. But we will not split theological hairs over it.

It appears that at the end of 1290 days his jurisdiction in the temple is over.

Does this mean that the Lord has come back at this time? Perhaps. It could also mean that other things prevail to move him out of this usurpation of abomination.

John in Revelation gives us more detail about this abomination of desolation.

I beheld another beast coming up out of the earth; and he had two horns like a lamb, and he spoke as a dragon [the Antichrist's companion, the False Prophet]. And he exerciseth all the power of the first beast before him, and causeth the earth and those who dwell therein to worship the first beast, whose deadly wound was healed. And he doeth great wonders, so that he maketh fire come down from heaven on the earth in the sight of men, and deceiveth them that dwell on the earth by means of thos miracles which he had power to do in the sight of the beast, saying to them that dwell on the earth that they should make an image of the beast which had the wound by the sword and did live. And he had power to give life unto the image of the beast, that the image of the beast should both speak and cause that as many as would not worship the image of the beast should be killed (Revelation 13:11-15).

The abomination of desolation is an image of the person of the Antichrist that is set up in the newly built Jewish temple. All people are told to worship this image.

Many will flee Jerusalem and Judea and Israel to the wilderness rather than worship or else refuse to worship and be killed for disobedience.

There is a prophetic theory which proposes that all of this was fulfilled in the year 162 B.C., when the infamous Jew-hater Antiochus Epiphanes offered a swine on the Jewish altar of the second temple.

But this was not the fulfillment, because decades later Jesus Christ Himself taught us to watch for the abomination of desolation that was to come, and for Jews to flee when they saw it.

Furthermore, when John wrote the Book of Revelation a number of years later, he declared what the abomination would be—the image of the Antichrist set up by the False Prophet in the temple.

Paul also wrote in 2 Thessalonians that the Man of Sin would claim to be the Messiah in this act of blasphemy. (This was more than two centuries after Antiochus Epiphanes performed his act of blasphemy.)

These prophecies are *future*, not historical.

THE ANTICHRIST PERSECUTES JEWS AND SAINTS, AND BLASPHEMES GOD AND HIS TEMPLE IN HEAVEN AND ON EARTH.

> *He opened his mouth in blasphemy against God, to blaspheme his name and his tabernacle and those that dwell in heaven. And it was given unto him to make war with the saints, and to overcome them; and power was given him over all kindreds and tongues and nations* (Revelation 13:6,7).

This is a tremendous revelation. The Antichrist curses God, Christ, and all in heaven. He knows they exist. His knowledge is great in theological matters.

He fights the saints and overcomes many of them. Where do these saints come from?

Certainly he will persecute the Jews who reject him, and he will persecute the Christians who despise him and his plans for world dominion and the worship of himself.

It is obvious, however, that his persecution of people, whatever kind, will be fiercer where he is located, and the closer populations to him will be the ones mostly molested by his troops and agents of death.

Israel and the Middle East nations will be scenes of terror for all who reject him.

Europe, both East and West, will fall as ready prey to his control.

Will the United States and Canada fall under his power? Quite probably, when we consider their need to trade with his Common Market. North America will need to trade with government number seven, and will be forced to cooperate with government number eight or else lose oil and thus energy needs.

As the Antichrist becomes government number eight, he will take over all oil and energy supplies of the Middle East.

> *He shall enter into the glorious land, and many countries shall be overthrown; but these shall escape out of his hand, even Edom*

> *and Moab and the chief of the children of Ammon. He shall stretch forth his hand also upon the countries; and the land of Egypt shall not escape* (Daniel 11:41,42).

When the Antichrist marches on Israel and when Jerusalem becomes his capital, he will take the neighboring countries gladly, for by then the oil wells could be rebuilt (after the terrible Soviet-Arab-Israeli-U.S.A. conflict is over).

He will then control the oil and will have his new international monetary system of the new credit card set up.

In order for the U.S. and Canada to trade with the Antichrist (which will be much needed in the aftermath of the war and/or great depression of the 80's), these countries will have to cooperate rather completely with the Antichrist and his regime.

Whether they will be called upon to worship him is debatable. His control in North America may be more monetary, industrial, and agricultural than spiritual.

However, either way, it is very possible that these twin nations will have to accept his new monetary system in order to buy or sell or undertake any kind of international commerce.

His persecution of Christians could mean the ones that will accept Jesus Christ as Lord and Savior in the aftermath of the miraculous deliverance from the Soviet-Arab war. Many will turn to God as He disciplines the earth in these mighty judgments.

The evangelical church is divided not so much on the coming of the Lord the second time at the end of the Battle of Armageddon as on the rapture question.

The rapture is the coming of Christ semisecretly in the clouds of the sky to catch away His own believers as they change from mortality to immortality, from corruption to incorruption, with their new bodies.

> *For the Lord Himself will descend from heaven with a shout, with the voice of the archangel and with the trumpet of God; and the dead in Christ shall rise first; then we which are alive and remain shall be caught up together with them in the clouds, to meet the Lord in the air, and so shall we ever be with the Lord. Wherefore comfort one another with these words* (1 Thessalonians 4:16-18).

It is such a marvelous comfort to Christians to know that Jesus Christ is coming and that He will snatch us up and out of this mundane sphere of living.

The question in evangelical minds is not *if* He is coming but *when*. If the Tribulation period of Daniel's seventieth week of years is seven years long, during which all hell will break loose on earth, will the rapture be pretribulational? Will the church vanish from the earth *before* the seven-year period, or will it remain and go *through* the Tribulation period on earth?

There are Biblical arguments for both views.

We do know that Christ is coming to earth at His second coming at the end of the seven-year period to end the Battle of Armageddon and set up His kingdom on earth.

But will He come in two stages? Will He first come *for* the saints (the church) and then come *with* the saints?

Without dividing your thoughts at this point, let me say to you that I *pray* for a *pre*tribulational rapture but *plan* for a *post*tribulational rapture.

I want a pretribulation rapture. Everyone who is alert to what is going to happen on the earth during the period would want that.

In the glossary at the end of the book I will give you the verses indicating both views, and leave the weight of evidence for you to decide.

If the rapture is pretribulational, then the saints whom the Antichrist will persecute through Europe, the Middle East, and North America will be Tribulation saints—who accepted Christ during this time.

If the rapture is *not* pretribulational, then the church would be involved in these persecutions to some extent.

Let us hope that the church will be gone. But if we are not gone, let not our faith waver, for:

> *He that endureth to the end shall be saved* (Matthew 10:22).

God will make provision for the church either way, for He said:

> *Because thou hast kept the word of my patience, I also will keep thee from the hour of temptation, which shall come upon all the world, to try them that dwell upon the earth. Behold, I come quickly: hold that fast which thou hast, that no man take thy crown* (Revelation 3:10,11).

He can "keep us from the hour of temptation (tribulation)" either by a pretribulation rapture or by His amazing grace in divine protection, as He did Israel coming out of Egypt.

The point is that millions of people will be persecuted and millions will be saved.

Remember that when Jesus Christ appears and destroys the Antichrist and his horde and the warring armies of earth, He then sets up the judgment of the living nations.

Millions of people evidently will not have taken the mark-of-the-Beast credit card or bowed down to the Antichrist or fought against Israel.

Had they all taken the mark, worshiped the Beast, or fought Israel, they would all be dead from God's judgment, and none would remain alive to go before Christ's judgment of the living nations.

Matthew 25:31-46 gives an account of millions who will not have worshiped the beast, taken his mark, or fought Israel.

It leaves us wondering how far the actual regime

of the Antichrist will reach.

THE ANTICHRIST WILL ESTABLISH A NEW MONETARY SYSTEM FOR HIS PART OF THE WORLD—A CREDIT CARD ON THE HAND OR FOREHEAD.

> *And he causeth all, both small and great, rich and poor, free and bond, to receive a mark in their right hand or in their foreheads; and that no man might buy or sell, except he that had the mark or the name of the beast or the number of his name. Here is wisdom. Let him that hath understanding count the number of the beast, for it is the number of a man; and his number is six hundred and sixty-six* (Revelation 13:16-18).

It is certainly not difficult for us to understand how this will be implemented as we look at sophisticated banking procedures in this electronic age of computerization.

The exact details of how the system will be set up we do not know (nor do we need to know), but the *fact* that all credit and buying and selling will be regulated by central banking and the one authority behind that is the main point.

There is no doubt in our minds that this central control, via a socialistic type of government out of Europe and the Middle East, will arrive on time. Satan has a timetable for the development of these major items.

We are already seeing many things leading up to

this. In the unified monetary system, suggested by the above verses, the world will be controlled by one single autocratic power, with headquarters other than in the United States.

Whether the "mark" will be visible to all or will be invisible and seen only through specialized equipment remains to be seen. If there is to be privacy for everyone regarding his own personal number, it may be invisible to the naked eye.

That would be a boon to Christians on earth at this time. They could exist by using what has been used universally for 6000 years—gold and silver, along with the barter method. They may also be "out of range" of the Antichrist inasmuch as they may be geographically too far away from him, or else God may protect them miraculously in a way and place as He has millions before them.

It appears that the mark may not be as universal as originally thought by theologians, for when Jesus Christ returns to the earth to terminate the enemies of Israel at the Battle of Armageddon and to wipe out the leaders and bring in everlasting righteousness (Matthew 25:31-46), He divides the "sheep" nations from the "goat" nations (the good from the bad) in what we commonly call "the judgment of the living nations."

Little is said in the Scriptures of this epochal event. We are led to some of our own reasoning in all the events surrounding these phenomenal days.

Is the possible scenario as follows?

A. The Antichrist is in Jerusalem usurping control of as much of the world as he can.

B. He forces individuals and nations to worship him and to bow down to him and take his "mark of allegiance," which enables the takers to buy and sell and live.

C. He cannot force all to do so. The Orientals may escape part of his wrath as they rise up and oppose him.

D. Armageddon begins and the battle is on.

E. Some individuals and nations resist him and will not take his mark or follow him. (There have to be many of these, for Revelation 20:4 teaches that there will be many resisting him, even unto death if necessary.)

F. Christ returns, and these saved ones are all resurrected and caught up to meet Him. At this time all redeemed are with Him, in glorified, incorruptible bodies, and their estate is fixed forever with Him.

G. Either the marriage and wedding supper are over, having taken place just prior to this moment of judgment, or else they will take place immediately after the judgment of the living nations. The point is that all of the redeemed appear to be immortal at this time.

H. Christ judges the living nations, with the

sheep nations (the good ones) on the right. The goat nations are on His left.

I. The sheep are allowed to enter into the millennial glory of the 1000 years of peace on earth.

J. The goats are consigned to everlasting punishment for their treatment of Israel and Christ's cause.

K. The millennial reign begins.

Would this mean that the sheep nations have not yet been regenerated, but are rejecters of the Antichrist and his mark? Quite possibly, or else who would be going into the millennial reign for the saints to govern and direct?

Who would repopulate the earth and give birth to babies and new civilizations for Christ to reign over, if all were either redeemed and now immortal or else were cast into hell?

1. There have to be many people who follow the Antichrist and take his mark, plus the ones fighting against him and then against Jesus Christ at His second coming. These are all destroyed at His coming.

2. There are those redeemed ones who were caught up and/or resurrected out of the Great Tribulation into heaven, joining others there for their change into immortality and the incorruptible body, awaiting the marriage supper of the Lamb.

3. There have to be those civilians who took the mark of the Beast upon themselves, who did not fight in Armageddon, but did follow the philosophy of the Antichrist. These are the "goat nations" and are consigned to perdition.

4. There are those individuals who did not accept Christ but who also did not accept the Antichrist or his mark. They held to the Judeo-Christian teachings to an extent and are rewarded with life and the opportunity of going into the millennial glory with Christ and His immortalized redeemed ones to repopulate and rebuild the earth.

Thus the teaching that not all will receive the Antichrist's mark.

What nations would resist him? Those having the greatest influence of Christianity in them, such as those in North America, who have accomplished the many things with regard to the principles of the Bible explained earlier in this book

THE ANTICHRIST TAKES OVER GOLD AND SILVER AND ESTABLISHES HIS OWN COMMERCIAL GODLESS SYSTEM IN THE EARTH—"BABYLON."

Daniel 11:42,43 indicates that the Antichrist will take over as much gold and silver as possible in the earth after he takes over Israel and the oil of the Middle East.

It could well be that the world is returned to

what monetarists call "the gold standard." He could back his new monetary system with the precious metals of the bimetallic past, when the U.S. and other nations of the world had a bimetallic backing for their monetary systems. It was gold backing for the paper dollar, which was guaranteed by the governments to be paid in gold and silver coinage on demand.

Most nations have dropped the bimetallic base for the monetary system and money supply of the nations.

In order to help bring allegiance to his monetary unit and unity throughout his empire, the Antichrist may try the bimetallic method again. (He also could just be greedily grabbing it all for himself.)

One point should be made here for Christians who want to survive the future depression and the economic collapse of the United States and other countries of the world. Gold and silver last in value and confidence and desirability above all paper monies, until the beginning of the Battle of Armageddon, and will not be judged until then (Revelation 18:1-12).

Both gold and silver are internationally recognized as the greatest stores of value for all times and troubles. It appears that God established it this way in the very beginning of Genesis and allows it to remain as sound Biblical economics until the end of time.

THE END OF THE ANTICHRIST AND HIS COM-

PANION IN CRIME, THE FALSE PROPHET, OC-
CURS AT THE SECOND COMING OF JESUS CHRIST.

Christ appears very close to the end of this battle of great bloodshed.

The Battle of Armageddon will at first involve the Antichrist and his followers in a pitched battle against the Orientals. They battle for some months and days, and finally, close to the end, when the enemy advances around Jerusalem (coming down from the Valley of Esdraelon in the northern part of Israel) Christ gloriously appears. His feet land on the Mount of Olives, and during all of this the enemies stop fighting one another and turn to fighting Him.

For a beautiful and complete description of His ascent, the battle, and His display of power, read Zechariah chapters 12 and 14 plus Revelation chapter 19. This will tell you the complete story of Christ's victory over the greatest evil known to mankind.

> *And I saw the beast, and the kings of the earth and their armies, gathered together to make war against him that sat on the horse, and against his army. And the beast was taken, and with him the false prophet that wrought miracles before him, with which he deceived them that had received the mark of the beast, and them that worshipped his image. These both were cast alive into a lake of fire burning with brimstone. And the rem-*

nant were slain with the sword of him that sat upon the horse, which sword proceeded out of his mouth; and all the fowls were filled with their flesh (Revelation 19:19-21).

GOD WILL DESTROY THE GODLESS COMMERCIALISM SET UP BY SATAN AND THE ANTICHRIST.

John saw two visions with respect to the term "Babylon." One was the great whore, representing all false religions in the earth since the beginning of time, during all world governments—religions that abandoned God and His will for the revelation of truth as it is revealed in His Word.

Thus Babylon is a derogatory term and was not a literal prostitute. But she represented all religions that prostituted the truth for material or political gain. She represented all religious organizations that hated the truth, disbelieved the truth, and committed spiritual adultery with the false principles of error rather than accept the truth.

Babylon can be many things with God. In Revelation 17 it is a woman, representing a religious system. In Revelation 18 it is a city, representing a godless commercial system carrying on business on the earth.

Both interpretations of Babylon involve systems. One is a religious system and the other is a commercial enterprise throughout the earth involving the human race.

Neither the city nor the woman are to be interpreted literally. Remember that symbolism was used of God with John to describe in perfect picture form the revelations that God was giving him.

It appears that Babylon the city is the symbol of all godless, dishonest commercialism throughout the earth that has been, is, and will be at that time. The crowning evil of Satan will be to place his chairman of the executive board of world government in place for the whole world to see.

Corruption, greed, dishonesty, avarice, murder, genocide, wars, deceptions, traitorous deeds, wicked deals, and evil machinations for all governments and businesses fall under this evil classification, and God can't wait to destroy it all in one hour!

Whether the "hour" is literal or not is inconsequential. God destroys all of this corruption as He destroys the satanic crowning glory over it—the Antichrist and his kingdom.

What rejoicing there will be in heaven as all who have been robbed, dishonestly treated, crushed, driven away, murdered for gain, or economically crippled will gaze upon a world paying its dues to the God of all love and honesty and holiness!

By this time God will have completed most of His judgments of earth for this time period.

> *For the former things have passed away. . . . Behold, I make all things new* (Revelation 21:4,5).

God will have brought about the end of all things that have displeased Him and that have brought grief to heaven up to this point in time.

The seven seals and their judgments have been opened and have brought an end to part of what God hated (Revelation 6:1—8:5).

The seven trumpets have sounded and have brought God's judgments on ecology, mankind, and nature (Revelation 8:6—10:11).

The seven thunders have sounded in judgment, and God would not let John tell us what they would be. But by now they are ended and have brought to a timely end all that God wanted destroyed by them (Revelation 10:1-4).

The seven vials of wrath have been poured out upon the earth during this time of the Antichrist. They have been poured out on the seat of the Antichrist's power and even upon the Euphrates River, making possible the coming of the Oriental hordes from the Far East into the Middle East (Revelation 16:1-21).

Now we have an end to:

1. All the revelations of the Person, work, and power of Jesus Christ (Revelation chapters 1 and 19).
2. The church age. No mention is made of the church in the Book of Revelation after chapter 3. Has she been raptured, represented by the 24 elders of chapter 4? We hope so, but if not, God protects her in part during the Tribulation period to be presented to Him at the time that pleases Him.

3. The end of the silence of heaven (Revelation 4 and 5). Heaven has become very much alive in the presence of God, with the 24 elders representing either the house of redeemed Israel from the Old Testament days or the raptured saints and the church up to that time. Either way, they are in heaven actively engaged in making their presence felt.
4. The end of perhaps as much as 25 percent of the world's population, including the Soviet Union and the militant Arabs (Revelation 6).
5. The end of Jewish rejection of Jesus Christ. A specially chosen 144,000 come to know Him (Revelation 7).
6. The end of world ecology through the judgments of God on a world that rejected His message of love (Revelation 8).
7. The end of world health, sanity, and common sense (Revelation 9).
8. The reference to the coming end of time (Revelation 10).
9. The end of the last two world evangelists (Revelation 11).
10. The end of Satan's jurisdiction over the atmospheric heavens and over Jewish control of Israel (Revelation 12).
11. The end of man's governments on earth and the establishment of government

number eight by the Antichrist (Revelation 13).

12. The end of man's civil liberties in the establishment of the mark of the beast on mankind (Revelation 15).

13. The end of the martyrs who are pictured in heaven. This is a picture of them all (Revelation 15).

14. The end of Oriental Communism—a picture of it as it begins at this time on the earth. The beginning of the Battle of Armageddon. The end of the Antichrist's peaceful period (Revelation 16).

15. The end of the great whore of Babylon. The false church is dead. This gives rise to the religion of the Antichrist (Revelation 17).

16. The end of the godless commercial Babylon of the world. The destruction of Babylon symbolized as a city (Revelation 18).

17. The end of the False Prophet and the Antichrist, and the end of the Battle of Armageddon (Revelation 19).

18. The end of Satan, sin, and sinners at the Great White Throne Judgment (Revelation 20).

19. The end of the world as we know it now, with its curse on nature (Revelation 21).

20. The end of the curse on mankind, nature, and everything cursed in the

Garden of Eden (Revelation 22).

These last three items of extreme importance have not as yet been destroyed in our ongoing list of fulfillments of the amazing prophecies of Scripture, but they will be destroyed shortly thereafter, at the end of Christ's millennial reign.

We can readily see how the Book of Revelation shows the end of it all and the new beginning of God's wonderful eternity.

6

Shockwaves of the Second Coming of Jesus Christ

After the Antichrist has moved to Israel and taken over the new and beautifully built temple of the Jews on Mount Moriah (where the Dome of the Rock has stood for years), there are rumblings from the Far East that trouble him.

> Tidings out of the east and out of the north shall trouble him; therefore he shall go forth with great fury to destroy, and utterly to make away many (Daniel 11:44).

The Antichrist will have planted the head-quarters of his eighth world government in the Holy Mountain, between the Mediterranean Sea on the west and the Dead Sea on the east. But now he is troubled that not all people respond to his demands.

Oriental Communists will never succumb to this white man and his one-world government ideology.

So they rebel. They rise up in forces never seen before, in waves of humanity perfectly equipped for the worst battle the world has ever known.

Revelation 9 alludes to the Euphrates River and an army of 200 million crossing over.

Revelation 16:12-16 adds to this truth by stating that they will cross over it and come to the land of Israel for the Battle of Armageddon.

Joel 3 tells us (as does Zechariah 12 and 14) of the coming of many Gentile armies to the Valley of Jehosaphat to battle against Jerusalem.

Revelation 14 states that when God thrusts in the sickle of His power the blood will run as high as the bridles of the horses for 160 miles! Could this be literal? Yes, if you include the bodies of the deceased and dying as indicated in Revelation 9.

> *The number of the army of the horsemen were two hundred million; and I heard the number of them. And thus I saw the horses in the vision, and them that sat on them, having breastplates of fire and jacinth and brimstone; and the heads of the horses were as the heads of lions, and out of their mouths issued fire and smoke and brimstone. By these three was the third part of men killed: by the fire and by the smoke and by the brimstone which issued out of their mouths.* (Revelation 9:16-18).

Yes, this could be an early-day description by the prophet of nuclear war. But whatever he saw in the vision, he was told the number of the army and the number of the dead.

Here in Revelation 9:18 John was told that a third of the population might die. Is this a third of the armies or a third of the world population? We do not know, but either way it is a tremendous number of casualties.

The Battle of Armageddon is to be much worse than the war with the Soviets, Arabs, and the armies of the Warsaw pact Forces of Europe.

One battle is before the seventieth week of Daniel's prophecy and the other ends it.

From all appearances the war starts with one motive and ends with another.

The motivating factor to begin Armageddon must be Oriental hatred of Occidental power in the world.

They hate this dictator of the Middle East and his ever-growing world government. He must have oppressed them to help motivate them to international war.

They would not gather together just to fight Jesus Christ in the beginning, for they do not believe in Him or His power or His second coming.

The Antichrist laughs at the theology and blasphemes heaven. The Oriental Communists, who are atheists, know nothing of His second coming. There has to be another motivating factor producing the Battle of Armageddon and the bloodshed even before the coming of the Son of Man in all His regal splendor.

As Communism in the Far East under Mao Tse-tung drove capitalism and the free-enterprise spirit out of mainland China to Formosa with its leaders and caused the mainland Chinese to hate the "imperialistic dogs of Americans" at that time, so this same hatred, fostered and encouraged by today's Chinese Communist leaders, will cause it to swell, grow, and fester into a painful boil that will cause them to believe that everything wrong about life in China with its privations is caused by the white man.

As sure as the Soviet Union will test its strength against the democracies of freedom and against God and truth, so the Communists of China will do the same, motivated by Satan himself.

I lived among Chinese in Hawaii for some time. It was my privilege to spend some time with them as members of the same faith in spiritual fellowship with the Lord and to learn of their relatives' hatred for the white man and the ultimate battle against the West by the East.

Not one of the Chinese community I knew ever doubted that this would come. All believed that brother would fight brother in order to gain the world for Communism.

Orientals control Hawaii for the most part. They made this part of my life and ministry refreshing and invigorating as we ministered among them in large hotel seminars and rallies. They are very astute members of the human race, and those that are Americanized (born here or educated here) love America and the opportunities afforded them, and are very industrious indeed.

I am impressed with the Christianized Chinese and Japanese that we have lived among and had fellowship with.

They, along with myself and many others, know that the masses of the Orientals do not know or understand Christianity. The masses of Chinese today were born under the regime of Mao and his Red Book Philosophy and Teachings.

He taught insidiously that to hate the white man and the noncommunist world was certain to bring great reward to any Chinese. He taught in his Red Book that they would conquer the white man in the battle to end all battles, and that Communism would cover the world—*Oriental* Communism and not Red Communism from Russia. He hated them almost as much as us!

There are over one billion Chinese living in mainland China today. Mao purged over 100 million of them during his time and tried to expunge from the memory of China (by rewriting the textbooks and closing the churches and schools) all histories of the past and all references to Christianity and the true history of China or any part of the world.

Most of today's population in China has been born since 1929 (when Mao started). He succeeded in 1949 in pushing the enemy to Formosa, and in 1959 he took over Tibet and colonized that land adjacent to China.

In the 1967 era and beyond, he closed the schools, universities, and churches of China. He burned the textbooks, purged the intellectuals by murder (through the infamous teenage army called the Red Guard), rewrote Chinese history, and replanned the education of the Chinese people. Part of that education was the further establishment of Communism, the hatred of the Western nations, and the ruthless dedication of millions to his principles.

For further documentation on the merciless way of life, the communal farms, the millions of lives lost, the division of families, and the establishment of Communism in China, write to the U.S. Government Printing Office and ask them for the $1.00 booklet entitled *The Human Cost of Communism in China.*

This government document, prepared by the CIA and the government of the United States and its Senators, will let you know why and how the Battle of Armageddon will come about.

It is the story of the East against the West. And for the U.S. government today to arm China to fight against Russia is really to arm China to fight against all of us eventually.

Perhaps it is inevitable that the very nations China is going to fight (i.e., the Western nations of Europe and North America) are falling over one another's feet to sell China on credit everything she needs to wage world war of such unprecedented proportions as to be gravely shocking to most prophecy students.

China perhaps will not be ready for that Battle of Armageddon in the decade of the 80's, *but maybe she will!*

Leading China experts, friends of mine in New York City studying Asian affairs in collaboration with the U.N., state that China will be ready toward the end of the 80's for this battle to end all battles.

The battle with Russia must come first. That is looming as the great future oil war, which is on the horizon right now.

How long the battle will rage we do not know, but some small indication is given us in Revelation in the same chapter that speaks of the 200 million soldiers.

> *Loose the four angels which are bound in the great river Euphrates. And the four angels were loosed, which were prepared for an hour and a day and month and a year to slay the third part of men* (Revelation 9:14,15).

This is a revelation of part of the fallen angels that fell when Lucifer was cast out of heaven and took a third part of the angels with him (Isaiah 14:12; Revelation 12:3,4).

Part of those angels were preserved to participate in God's plan for the end time.

In Revelation 16:12-16 it appears that demonic fallen angels participate in stirring up the nations for war.

> *The sixth angel poured out his vial upon the*

> *great river Euphrates, and the water thereof was dried up, that the way of the kings of the east might be prepared. And I saw three unclean spirits like frogs come out of the mouth of the dragon, and out of the mouth of the beast, and out of the mouth of the false prophet. For they are the spirits of devils, working miracles which go forth unto the kings of the earth and of the whole world, to gather them to the battle of that great day of God Almighty. Behold, I come as a thief. Blessed is he that watcheth, and keepeth his garments, lest he walk naked, and they see his shame. And he gathered them together into a place called in the Hebrew tongue Armageddon* (Revelation 16:12-16).

This is a very vivid description of a symbolic vision which John saw of the demons instigating the nations to fight.

It appears that they come to fight one another but then turn to fight the Lord Jesus Christ and His armies.

CHRIST RETURNS WITH THE ARMIES OF HEAVEN TO CONQUER ALL WHO OPPOSE GOD AND HIS WILL, AND TO ESTABLISH THE KINGDOM OF GOD ON EARTH.

He comes, but not alone.

Armies from heaven descend with Him to the skies and then to the earth for battle with the enemy.

The armies are only symbolical of Christ's

power, though they may be literal enough. The power that grinds the enemies to the ground is the Word of His mouth—the sharp sword of the Word of the living God.

This is enough to destroy the enemy. Christ needs no accomplice to aid Him in the destruction of His foes.

In all His regal splendor He enters the atmospheric heavens with such dignity, such power, such undeniable divinity, and such immeasurable glory as to suddenly stun the shocked inhabitants of the earth.

The brilliance of His second coming dethrones earthly reason, destroys earth's warring ambitions, and devastates the plans of all humans as they gaze in suspended animation upon Him while listening to the voice of a million angels sing a chorus of hallelujahs that reverberates throughout the streets, the cities, and the corridors of earth from the highest pinnacle to the lowest cavern sheltering fearful Jews in Petra.

The vastness of His appearance, the immeasurable brightness, and the infiniteness of His boundless glory impregnate earthlings with a paralysis of spirit so intense that it renders them immovable objects of His justified wrath.

Earth's immovable objects are pinned to the ground. Millions gaze as the Mount of Olives splits in two, careening wildly right to the top, from the floor of the Garden of Gethsemene.

They look up from all over the world to see the

sky lit up brilliantly, with every conceivable color in the rainbow blending into harmonious hues of marvelous tones.

The heavens seem to be opening up with such brilliance that the armies on earth are pinned to the ground immovable.

"Every eye shall see Him."

No one will miss this occasion. Every leaf will be silent. Not a breeze will blow, nor a tree move, nor beast of the field, nor bird of the air.

The raptured ones will be with Christ, as will be the resurrected saints from the dead. They are clothed in white, the righteousness of the saints. They constitute the armies of the Lord Jesus Christ and shout as He passes through the air in complete victory.

For whatever time is necessary, the earthly members of the human family gaze upon the celestial glory that threatens to destroy them or capture them.

According to Bible prophecy, by this time all the redeemed will be with Christ at His return.

> *As in Adam all die, even so in Christ shall all be made alive. But every man in his own order: Christ the firstfruits; afterward they that are Christ's at His coming. Then cometh the end, when He shall have delivered up the kingdom to God, even the Father, when he shall have put down all authority and power; for he must reign till he hath put all enemies under his feet* (1 Corinthians 15:22-25).

All groups of believers from the Old Testament and New Testament days are present.

The 24 elders are there, along with the four living creatures.

The 144,000 chosen Jews are there, clothed in immortality, along with the innumerable host that that were resurrected out of the Great Tribulation, who lost their lives in the wars and devastation.

The redeemed of Israel and the redeemed of the Gentile nations are all one.

The martyrs have their new bodies and have long forgotten the butchery, their inhumane deaths, and the torturous slayings of their loved ones with them.

The souls under the altar are redeemed and clothed, and are singing the songs of eternity forever.

There are seven groups constituting the final glorious number of redeemed beings making up the first resurrection.

1. The 24 elders (Revelation 4:4-11).
2. The four living creatures (Revelation 4:6-9).
3. The souls under the altar (Revelation 6:9-11).
4. The 144,000 chosen Jews (Revelation 7:4-8).
5. The innumerable host of Gentiles (Revelation 7:9,10).
6. The martyrs (Revelation 15:1-4).
7. The tribulation saints (Revelation 19:1-4).

By the time we get to Revelation 19, all the redeemed are in heaven—raptured, translated, caught up, and resurrected completely.

There is only one resurrection which is incomplete, and that is the resurrection of the unjust at the Great White Throne Judgment of God.

As to how, when, and under what circumstances all seven groups of the redeemed make it to heaven, we will have to leave this with God, knowing that He does all things well.

The saints who rejected the mark of the Beast and who refused to bow down to worship the image of the Antichrist are now clothed with immortality. All of Christ's chosen ones are there. What an indescribably glorious reunion and celebration of victory!

Christ then destroys the Antichrist, the False Prophet, and the armies of the lost (Revelation 19:17-20).

CHRIST SETS UP THE JUDGMENT OF THE LIVING NATIONS (MATTHEW 25:31-46).

All nations come before Him. Whether gradually or in some quick and miraculous way, He judges them.

The goats on the left are those who:

1. Mistreated the Jews and Israel.
2. May have worshiped the Antichrist.
3. May have taken the mark of the Beast.
4. Opposed the gospel of Jesus Christ.
5. Are assigned to hell forever.

The nations, families, and individuals on the right did the opposite:

A. They are not necessarily saved, for the saved from this period are now immortalized at Christ's coming, with the dead resurrected. All are in the air with Him, coming back as His saints and as His armies.

B. They did not oppose Israel or the Jews in any way.

C. They befriended Israel and the Jews in every way.

D. They were humanitarian to all.

E. They may not be Christian in the sense of knowing salvation, but they did not take the mark of the Beast.

F. They did not worship the Beast.

G. They did not follow the Beast.

JEWS SHALL LOOK UPON HIM AND GO INTO MOURNING.

In addition to the armies of the aliens plus the followers of the Antichrist and Satan seeing Christ and being destroyed by Him at the brightness of His coming, *the Jews* will see Him in His brilliance and deity.

> *It shall come to pass in that day that I will seek to destroy all the nations that come against Jerusalem. And I will pour upon the house of David and upon the inhabitants of Jerusalem the spirit of grace and supplica-*

tions; and they shall look upon me whom they have pierced, and they shall mourn for him as one mourneth for his only son, and shall be in bitterness for him as one that is in bitterness for his for his firstborn (Zechariah 12:9,10).

His feet shall stand in that day upon the Mount of Olives, which is before Jerusalem on the east; and the Mount of Olives shall cleave in the midst thereof toward the east and toward the west, and there shall be a very great valley; and half of the mountain shall remove toward the north, and half of it toward the south. . . . And it shall be in that day that living waters shall go out from Jerusalem: half of them toward the former sea and half of them toward the hinder sea; in summer and in winter shall it be. And the Lord shall be King over all the earth (Zechariah 14:4,8,9).

Blindness in part is happened to Israel until the fulness of the Gentiles be come in. And so all Israel shall be saved, as it is written, There shall come out of Zion the Deliverer, who shall turn away ungodliness from Jacob; for this is my covenant unto them, when I shall take away their sins (Romans 11:25-27).

God brings salvation to the house of Israel at the second coming of Christ.

A miraculous spirit of supplication, prayer, and repentance falls upon them as a nation, for they as the true vine are grafted back into the olive tree with the Lord (Romans chapters 9-11).

God lets their blinded eyes see the glories of Jesus Christ, but instead of rejoicing that their King has finally arrived, they realize immediately what they have done in rejecting Him. They repent and mourn over their 2000-year national error and over their own personal sins.

Christ opens a fountain of cleansing for them at this moment, and all Israel is saved.

They enter the millennial reign with Jesus Christ and His reigning saints, along with the unregenerate that He allows into His new kingdom.

Thus there are three types of beings in the kingdom era— 1) Christ with His immortalized beings (who were redeemed, raptured, and/or resurrected before this kingdom age), 2) redeemed Jews in the house of David, and 3) the nations to be evangelized, who will help rebuild the world under the supervision of God's redeemed people for 1000 years.

For further references on Christ's second coming see Matthew 24:27; 25:31-46; Luke 21:28,36; Acts 1:11; 1 Corinthians 15:51-56; Philippians 3:20,21; Colossians 3:4; 1 Thessalonians 4:16-18; 2 Thessalonians 2:1-8; 1 Timothy 6:13-15; 2 Timothy 4:1; Titus 2:11-14; Hebrews 9:27,28; James 5:7,8; 1 Peter 5:4; 2 Peter 3:1-13; 1 John 3:1-3; Revelation 1:7; 3:10,11; 16:15; 22:12,20.

All of these verses teach clearly the bodily return of the Lord Jesus Christ to the clouds of the sky and then to the earth, where His feet will touch down on the Mount of Olives.

THE MARRIAGE SUPPER OF THE LAMB AND BRIDE.

This marvelous act for the church, the bride of Christ, takes place in heaven just before the final activities of destroying the Antichrist and the final moments of the Battle of Armageddon.

Before Christ appears to the world (when all the redeemed of all ages have been caught up to Him, "every man in his order"), heaven has the greatest of all celebrations up to this point.

Revelation 19 indicates that the saints are in heaven, singing and rejoicing as the final members of God's chosen people arrive from out of the Tribulation for the festivities.

The church is united with her glorious Lord and Savior who made her redemption possible by His death.

No doubt this is also the time of the judgment of works for believers, as they are rewarded for all the wonderful deeds done in Christ's name and for His glory.

Great will be the celebrations in this celestial scene, when the rewards for labors around the world are given and the "church is presented without spot or wrinkle to the One who died to redeem it"!

Then comes the Battle of Armageddon.

7

The Infinite World to Come

The world predicted to come is not far off in terms of actual years, months, and days!

Prophecy is like a giant puzzle that God has given man to try to put together. Without the Holy Spirit in our heart and without a regenerated soul, we cannot begin to understand the mysteries of the puzzle.

Even then, with regeneration and the leadership of the Holy Spirit, God never seems to reveal all prophetic truth to any one man. That would not be good for our ego or our spirituality!

The Apostle Paul in 2 Corinthians 12:1-7, was caught up into the third heaven and saw revelations of things that were unspeakable; he could not utter them or understand them.

He saw heaven and the angels; eternity was revealed to this mighty man of God. He caught a vision of absolute perfection and called it paradise.

Lest he become exalted above measure, a "thorn in the flesh" was given him to keep him submissive to God and to keep him from being exalted above measure. Paul too was a man, sensitive to the emotions of a man, including the emotion of pride.

God doesn't let any of us see all truth at any one stage of our life. We are a family. The family of God all have the opportunity of seeing into divine truths and learning from one another.

The greatest of theologians (and some of them very humble men who walked with God) were divided on some theological issues in the past, and this is still true today.

But God loves us all. The puzzle continues to be a puzzle, but the more we study it and love it and pray about it, the more the Lord loves to reveal it to us (1 Corinthians 2:7-16).

CHRIST ENTERS JERUSALEM BY THE EASTERN GATE THAT HAS BEEN SHUT FOR HUNDREDS OF YEARS.

A new Jerusalem is built, to which the nations will come during the millennial reign for worship and to make pilgrimages to the feet of Christ.

> *Then he brought me back the way of the gate of the outward sanctuary which looketh toward the east, and it was shut. Then said the Lord unto me, This gate shall be shut; it shall not be opened, and no man shall enter in by it, because the Lord, the God of Israel, hath entered in by it; therefore it shall be*

shut. It is for the prince; the prince shall sit in it to eat bread before the Lord (Ezekiel 44:1-3).

For many decades the Eastern Gate, commonly called the Golden Gate, has been closed in the wall around the City of Jerusalem. It is seemingly a fulfillment of this ancient prophecy. Christ will open it as He enters the city at His appearance.

Ezekiel chapters 40-48 seem to be a description of Jerusalem and the temple area that Christ will enjoy and utilize during His millennial reign of 1000 years.

The temple area and the area for the priests is immense, and the ultimate fulfillment of these many chapters will come during the millennial reign.

The best teachings of God's Word on the period come from Revelation 20 and the entire Book of Isaiah. (Isaiah was a millennial prophet indeed!)

And I saw an angel come down from heaven, having the key of the bottomless pit and a great chain in his hand. And he laid hold on the dragon, that old serpent which is the Devil and Satan, and bound him a thousand years, and cast him into the bottomless pit, and shut him up, and set a seal upon him, that he should deceive the nations no more till the thousand years should be fulfilled; and after that he must be loosed a little season. And I saw thrones, and they sat upon them, and judgment was given unto them; and I saw the souls of them that were beheaded for the witness of Jesus, and for the word of God, and which had not worshipped the beast nor his image, neither had received his mark upon their foreheads or in their hands; and they lived and reigned with Christ a thousand years. But the rest of the dead lived not again until the thousand years were finished. This is the first resurrection. Blessed and holy is he that hath part in the first resurrection; on such the second death hath no power, but they shall be priests of God and of Christ, and shall reign with him a thousand years. And when the thousand years are expired, Satan shall be loosed out of his prison, and shall go out to deceive the nations which are in the four quarters of the earth, Gog and Magog, to gather them together to battle, the number of whom is as the sand of the sea. And they went up on the breadth of the earth, and compassed the camp of the saints about, and the beloved city; and fire came down from God out of heaven, and devoured them. And the Devil that deceived them was cast into the lake of fire and brimstone, where the beast and false prophet are, and shall be tormented day and night for ever and ever (Revelation 20:1-10).

No less than six times in this passage the

1000-year period is specifically referred to as a literal period of time.

Peter gives us a very interesting explanation of the various periods of thousands of years since the beginning of time and reminds us that one year with the Lord is as one day, and one day as a thousand years (2 Peter 3:1-13, esp. v. 8).

The idea is that the earth has labored under death, the curse, wars, etc. for six days. Now it is the seventh day, and it is time to rest, even as God made the world in six days and rested on the seventh.

It is time for the earth to rest and for God's people to enter into His rest (Hebrews 4:1-11).

The general teaching of Scripture indicates clearly that God's world will rest for one day, or one thousand years, and then very special things will happen on the earth and in the atmospheric heavens above the earth.

We learn the following important truths from Revelation 20.

1. Satan will be bound during this period so that the earth can rest from sin, unrighteousness, and evil, which is the rule of living today.

2. While Satan is bound, peace will abound on earth. There will be no war, and the increase of Christ's judgment and peace there will be no end.

> *Of the increase of his government and peace there shall be no end, upon the throne of David and upon his kingdom, to order it and to establish it with judgment and with justice from henceforth even for ever. The zeal of the Lord of hosts will perform this* (Isaiah 9:7).

Christ will have direct control over the whole earth. To His redeemed saints in their new bodies, and to the house of Israel who have been redeemed and remain in their human bodies, He gives special powers to govern.

Revelation 20 states that they are on thrones and that judgment is given to them. The world needs ruling, and they have the privilege and responsibility to do this.

> *He that overcometh, and keepeth my works unto the end, to him will I give power over the nations; and he shall rule them with a rod of iron; as the vessels of a potter shall they be broken to shivers* (Revelation 2:26,27).

The saints will rule the world in judgment as led by the Lord Himself.

> *Do you not know that the saints shall judge the world?* (1 Corinthians 6:2).

How this will be enacted is not revealed, but the many promises of the Word indicate that we will participate in governing all over the earth, Christianizing the nations.

WAR WILL BE ENDED AND THE NATIONS WILL FLOW INTO JERUSALEM IN HOLY PIMGRIMAGES.

> *It shall come to pass in the last days that the mountain of the Lord's house shall be established in the top of the mountains, and shall be exalted above the hills; and all nations shall flow unto it. And many people shall go and say, Come, let us go up to the mountain of the Lord, to the house of the God of Jacob; and he will teach us of his ways, and we will walk in his paths; for out of Zion shall go forth the law, and the word of the Lord from Jerusalem. And he shall judge among the nations, and shall rebuke many people; and they shall beat their swords into plowshares, and their spears into pruning hooks; nation shall not lift up sword against nation, neither shall they learn war anymore (Isaiah 2:2-4).*

This is one of the most beautiful passages of prophecy concerning the millennial reign, the authority of the saints, the power of the risen Lord, and the peace that shall come to the world.

HAPPINESS, PEACE, AND HOLINESS WILL RETURN TO JERUSALEM AND THE WHOLE EARTH.

> *Thus saith the Lord: I am returned unto Zion, and will dwell in the midst of Jerusalem; and Jerusalem shall be called a city of truth, and the mountain of the Lord of hosts, The holy*

*mountain. Thus saith the Lord of hosts:
There shall yet old men and old women dwell
in the streets of Jerusalem, and every man
with his staff in his hand for very age. And
the streets of the city shall be full of boys and
girls playing in the streets thereof* (Zechariah
8:3-5).

EQUITY AND JUSTICE WILL RETURN TO THE
EARTH, WITH CHRIST REIGNING AND HIS
SAINTS SUPERVISING.

*For the seed shall be prosperous: The vine
shall give her fruit, and the ground shall give
her increase, and the heavens shall give their
dew; and I will cause the remnant of this people to possess all these things. . . . These are
the things that ye shall do: Speak every man
the truth to his neighbor; execute the judgment of truth and peace in your gates; and let
none of you imagine evil in your hearts
against his neighbor; and love no false oath;
for all these are things that I hate, saith the
Lord* (Zechariah 8:12,16,17).

Holy living, honesty, kindness, and charitable at-
titudes will return to the earth, along with genuine
friendship of neighbor for neighbor. Imagine a
truly friendly, loving world with virtually no sin
or thoughts of sin!

JEWS WILL LEAD THE WORLD TO CHRIST
AND HIS PEACE AND LOVE.

*The inhabitants of one city shall go to
another, saying, Let us go speedily to pray*

> *before the Lord, and to seek the Lord of hosts;*
> *I will go also. Yea, many people and strong*
> *nations shall come to seek the Lord of hosts*
> *in Jerusalem, and to pray before the Lord.*
> *Thus saith the Lord of hosts: In those days it*
> *shall come to pass that ten men shall take*
> *hold out of all languages of the nations, even*
> *shall take hold of the skirt of him that is a*
> *Jew, saying, We will go with you, for we have*
> *heard that God is with you* (Zechariah
> 8:21-23).

What a switch! The world once hated Jews. Now
they will hold to them, knowing that the Lord
dwells in their Holy City. Redeemed Israel will
help evangelize the world and will keep the law
and order of Christ's peace for this memorable
time.

LONG LIFE WILL ONCE AGAIN BE HERE TO EN-
JOY. DEATH WILL NOT COME EARLY. SINNERS
WILL BE THE EXCEPTION TO THE RULE. A CAR-
NIVOROUS SPIRIT WILL NO LONGER BE INNATE
TO ANIMALS.

> *The wolf also shall dwell with the lamb, and*
> *the leopard shall lie down with the kid; and*
> *the calf and the young lion and the fatling*
> *together; and a little child shall lead them.*
> *And the cow and the bear shall feed; their*
> *young ones shall lie down together; and the*
> *lion shall eat straw like the ox. And the suck-*
> *ling child shall play on the hold of the asp,*
> *and the weaned child shall put his hand on*

> *the cockatrice's den. They shall not hurt nor destroy in all my holy mountain, for the earth shall be full of the knowledge of the Lord as the waters cover the sea* (Isaiah 11:6-9).

Animals that are now flesh-eaters will no longer have the carnivorous lust within them.

Children and babies can play with what today would be considered poisonous reptiles and insects. In that day these will not hurt them at all.

Animals that today are hostile to one another will eat and live together in perfect harmony.

Isaiah 35 seems to be a song about the very things that other chapters speak of in prose. The prophet exalts the Lord and sings of healing of the blind, the deaf, and the lame.

The earth will bring forth abundantly without excruciating labor.

The curse will not have been lifted entirely, but certainly mankind will have things much easier during this glorious period.

The biological functions of the human body will remain, and children will be born, who are to be evangelized by the Lord's redeemed people as the children grow to maturity.

DEATH WILL OCCUR MUCH LATER IN LIFE, AS IN THE DAYS OF ADAM. THERE WILL BE SOCIAL JUSTICE FOR ALL PEOPLE, BUT WITHOUT COMMUNISM OR SOCIALISM.

> *There shall be no more an infant of days, nor an old man that hath not filled his days, for*

the child shall die a hundred years old; but the sinner being a hundred years old shall be accursed. And they shall build houses, and inhabit them, and they shall plant vineyards and eat the fruit of them. They shall not build, and another inhabit; they shall not plant, and another eat; for as the days of a tree are the days of my people, and mine elect shall long enjoy the work of their hands. They shall not labor in vain, nor bring forth for trouble; for they are the seed of the blessed of the Lord, and their offspring with them. . . . The wolf and the lamb shall feed together, and the lion shall eat straw like the bullock; and dust shall be the serpent's meat. They shall not hurt nor destroy in all my holy mountain, saith the Lord (Isaiah 65:20-25).

This is one of the most glowing passages in all of Isaiah, and the prophet must have felt genuine exultation for the Lord and the promised world to come as he wrote such inspired words about our future world.

Length of days would return to the human race, giving us further expansion on the truth that humans functioning as biological beings will be in the millennial world. They will produce offspring, as the passage distinctly says.

Death will not be totally done away with, but it will be primarily for the sinner, in his younger years, and even that will be over 100 years of age. When the saints die, as they evidently will (that is, people regenerated to the Lord during this period—not the redeemed saints in their immortal bodies), they will be considered dying in infancy if they die at 100 years of age!

Commerce will go on, but this time in honesty and justice. A person will not build a house but then have to give it to another person. People will plant and eat and enjoy the fruit of their labors in a world perfectly governed by Christ's representatives.

It should be pointed out that this will not be an absolutely perfect time, for the very fact that the saints will judge, govern, and oversee the world indicates that there will be problems to judge, oversee, and make right.

But imagine the world turned morally, religiously, and philosophically upside down from what it is now. That is what the world will be like then.

Now we have dishonest governments and courts, a justice system that is weak, and a judiciary that is spineless.

Then we will have a perfect government, one that makes no mistakes in dealing with men everywhere. It will be right, but it will be firm and proper as well as kind.

Now we have sickness and disease killing the human family. Then we will have healing, curing, little death by error, none by war, and little if any by killing.

Now we have courts, police, medicine, hunger, homelessness, floods, famine, and natural disasters. Then the earth will rest from most if not all of the natural phenomena. There will be plenty of food but no implements needed for war, so everything will be for the good of the human race.

Legislative bodies will be run totally by the saints and the redeemed of the house of Israel.

The Bible speaks of the "nations." Obviously there will be some self-rule. But it will be under the guiding authority of the King in Jerusalem and His emissaries of love.

The world will feel the impact of His love but also the infiniteness of His power and honest government for this wonderful period. It is hard for us to imagine it!

SWEEPING CHANGES WILL TAKE PLACE IN THIS EPOCHAL PERIOD OF THE FUTURE.

1. This will be the golden age, with new social, judicial, ethical, and free-enterprise establishments.

Isaiah calls it the "new earth," and states that the former earth will not be remembered (Isaiah 65:17).

This is the age of utopia that so many people have looked for, longed for, and through a variety of religious philosophies striven for.

Every need of humanity and every cry from the earth for anything will be answered and met in great sufficiency from and by the hand of the Lord.

"Before they call, I will answer" (Isaiah 65:24). God will be aware of the previous social injustices and inequities, and in this world and age He will do everything divinely possible to bring the complete changes necessary to make this the millennial reign.

> *Wisdom and knowledge shall be the stability of thy times, and strength of salvation; the fear of the Lord is his treasure* (Isaiah 33:6).

Salvation will be abundantly available to the nations of mankind, who saw the end of the Antichrist and the False Prophet. They saw the coming of the Lord in the heavens. They now have opportunities to accept Him personally, even as you and I have right now.

It will be a wonderful spiritual kingdom (Joel 2:28).

> *With joy shall ye draw water out of the wells of salvation* (Isaiah 12:3).

> *He hath clothed me with the garments of salvation* (Isaiah 61:10).

> *The Lord hath made bare His holy arm in the eyes of all nations; and all the ends of the earth shall see the salvation of our God* (Isaiah 52:10).

So much of the Bible and so much of life is full of suffering because of the world we live in, and so much of our time is filled with recovering from the ills of the age and from the wickedness that surrounds us. Therefore it is only fitting that many verses of at least one book of the Bible should tell us about the golden age of utopia to come soon.

Isaiah is the prophet of the millennial reign, although several others also touch on the promises of the wonderful events to come.

The reason this is so important to us now is that we are going to see it transpire relatively soon!

Many verses are there for your consideration dealing with the spiritual life of the people and nations. Salvation and spiritual power will be evident everywhere. A beautiful evening study will enable you and yours to see how spiritually fruitful this day will be as you study the following passages: Psalm 45; 98; 145; Zechariah 12:10; Jeremiah 31:9; Isaiah 55:4-7; Micah 7:19; Ezekiel 36:24-38; Zephaniah 3:11-13; Isaiah 32:1,2; 51:11; 55:1-3; 60:21; 61:2,3.

2. Christ will be the international authority, and of course Jerusalem will be the world capital. (Isaiah 2:3; Ezekiel 43:1-7; Psalm 110:2).

The Jewish problem will be forever solved. The Jews will inhabit the land from Egypt to Assyria (Ezekiel 37:21,22). Israel will enjoy a spiritual revival and will gain all the land from the Euphrates River southward—land that she once had in the days of her forefathers, without the current dispute of nations.

3. It is even possible that we will have one international language. A wonderful verse in Zephaniah says this:

> Then will I turn to the peoples a pure language, that they may all call upon the

*name of the Lord, to serve him with one con-
sent* (Zephaniah 3:9).

It appears that one language may be given to all
people as part of the curse is lifted. The division of
languages came as a result of the sins of Babel
(Babylon), and now they are destroyed. The earth
could revert back to its original unity of language.
It is a beautiful thought.

4. There will be beneficial and wonderful
changes in the climates and vegetation throughout
the earth.

It appears that even weather patterns will
change in this millennial world. Great cosmic and
geological changes will transpire during the
Tribulation period. Earthquakes will jolt the
world, remove mountains, fill valleys with water,
and destroy cities in a day, in an hour. Ecological
changes will shift the earth and also change the
earth (Revelation chapter 9). Uncanny events will
come as a result of God's judgment on nature that
will affect the living conditions of mankind.

When judgment strikes, nature will be the tool
of God to effect judgments and changes in the
earth upon those rejecting God's love.

God will have complete control of nature and
will bless the world with its abundant pleasures
during the millennial reign of Christ.

> *The light of the moon shall be as the light of
> the sun, and the light of the sun shall be
> sevenfold, as the light of seven days, in the*

day that the Lord bindeth up the breach of his people, and healeth the stroke of their wound (Isaiah 30:26).

Cosmic changes will fill the earth, and the earth's agricultural productivity will be phenomenal (Isaiah 30:22-25).

Abundant rainfall is promised (See also Joel 2:21-24; Isaiah 30:25):

In the wilderness shall waters break out, and streams in the desert. And the parched ground shall become a pool, and the thirsty land springs of water (Isaiah 35:6,7).

Wonderful promises strongly suggest that the earth's productivity will vastly increase. It is bound to, with so much money and wealth going for the production of peaceful causes instead of death-producing machinery.

The wilderness and the dry land shall be glad, and the desert shall rejoice, and blossom as the rose (Isaiah 35:1).

5. Famine will be gone from the earth (Ezekiel 34:29). Sickness and disease will be immediately cured (Isaiah 35:5,6; Isaiah 33:24). A special kind of medicine will come from the Dead Sea for healing. The Dead Sea will become filled with fish.

It shall come to pass that the fishers shall stand upon it from Engedi to Eneglaim; there shall be a place to spread forth nets; their fish shall be according to their kinds, as the fish of the great sea, exceeding many. . . . And

> *by the river upon the bank thereof, on this side and on that side, shall grow all trees for food, whose leaf shall not fade, neither shall the fruit thereof be consumed: it shall bring forth new fruit according to its months, because their waters issued out of the sanctuary; and the fruit thereof shall be for food, and the leaf thereof for medicine* (Ezekiel 47:10-12).

The Dead Sea is over 33 percent salt and minerals now, and as the fish come from the Sea of Galilee down through the Jordan River and eventually into the Dead Sea, they immediately die of the minerals and salt.

This prophecy indicates that the fishermen will fish the Dead Sea, and an earlier prophecy indicates that waters will flow from the City of Jerusalem to the "Hinder Sea."

These waters will act as an artesian flow so powerful as to neutralize the salinity and minerals of the Dead Sea, thereby making fishing possible.

This is not the only miracle. Has God been preparing the basic minerals needed to help bring about healing from the Dead Sea, healing that will only be effective during the millennial reign?

The river that flows from the City of Jerusalem produces vegetation (in the form of fruit trees on both sides of the river) that will provide superior nourishment for the people. Also, the leaves of the tree have some ingredients for the healing of the nations (at least Israel).

It is interesting to note that the healing word for medicine is used, indicating that there will be sickness, diseases, etc., but that this leaf will have healing in it.

Not only will the divine power of our Lord be demonstrated as it was in the days of His first coming, but He will use nature in the form of medicine for healing.

> *Every good gift and every perfect gift is from above, and cometh down from the Father of lights, with whom is no variableness nor shadow of turning* (James 1:17).

Herbs, medicines, and God's wisdom for today can be helpful right now. Satan has never given the human race any cures for sickness and disease. Only God in His love gave us medical science. Whether it is always as good as we wish is not the point. Whether all physicians practice properly is not the point. The wisdom behind medicine came from above.

God will allow earthly practitioners to practice medicine during the millennial reign under His divine guidance and rules.

6. Physical safety and many hazards of nature and living will be reduced or eliminated.

Millions today lose their lives in tornadoes, hurricanes, vehicle accidents, and a host of daily occurences that take lives through the natural hazards of life and living.

The verses from Isaiah chapters 11 and 65 clearly

indicate that wild animals will no longer be ferocious. People will no longer be attacked by these creatures.

Psalm 91 appears to have millennial overtones in it.

> *There shall no evil befall thee, neither shall any plague come nigh thy dwelling, for he shall give his angels charge over thee, to keep thee in all thy ways. They shall bear thee up in their hands, lest thou dash thy foot against a stone* (Psalm 91:10-12).

7. Jerusalem will be the home of the Lord Jesus Christ. His will be a perfect rule, and He will use saints to accomplish His will. Another temple will be erected to His glory and will be the focal point of the nations.

> *Mine house shall be called a house of prayer for all people* (Isaiah 56:7).

> *For Zion's sake I will not hold my peace, and for Jerusalem's sake I will not rest, until the righteousness thereof go forth as brightness, and the salvation thereof as a lamp that burneth. And the Gentiles shall see thy righteousness, and all kings thy glory* (Isaiah 62:1,2).

> *The glory of the Lord came into the house by the way of the gate whose prospect is toward the east. So the Spirit took me up and brought me into the inner court, and, behold, the glory*

of the Lord filled the house. And I heard him speaking unto me out of the house, and the man stood by me. And he said unto me, Son of man, the place of my throne and the place of the soles of my feet, where I will dwell in the midst of the children of Israel forever, and my holy name, shall the house of Israel no more defile, neither they nor their kings by their whoredom, nor by the carsasses of the kings in their high places. ... Thou son of man, show the house to the house of Israel (Ezekiel 43:4-10).

Even rabbis and Jews of the house of Judaism today agree that this is a kingdom-age temple and a revelation of God's presence. Nothing like this has ever taken place, so they say, "It is not history; it must be prophecy."

Ezekiel tells us of the return of the Jew to the land in chapters 36 and 37. Then he tells us of the coming war with Magog and the satellite nations with her in chapter 38. We next learn of their demise in the hills of Israel in chapter 39.

Then the prophet tells us of this holy temple in chapters 40 to 48. It was immediately after chapter 39 that he entered into the revelation of the Lord concerning a temple never built before or since. In chapters 40 to 48 we have the dimensions, order, and return of the glory of the Lord to an earthly temple.

The dimensions and details of the temple as

given in Ezekiel will require a great change in the topography of the land. All of this will take place during the events described earlier in this book.

Lest you be confused by Ezekiel's predictions about the new temple and the reestablishment of some blood sacrifices, remember that even today we take the cup and bread in remembrance of Him and His death, and His coming again.

8. Israel will be part of the main thrust of evangelism at this time. The glorified saints will govern more than evangelize.

> *The Spirit of the Lord God is upon me, because the Lord hath anointed me to preach good tidings unto the meek; he hath sent me to bind up the broken-hearted, to proclaim liberty to the captives and the opening of the prison to them that are bound; to proclaim the acceptable year of the Lord, and the day of vengeance of our God; to comfort all that mourn; to appoint unto them that mourn in Zion, to give unto them beauty for ashes, the oil of joy for mourning, the garment of praise for the spirit of heaviness, that they might be called trees of righteousness, the planting of the Lord, that he might be glorified. ... But ye shall be named the priests of the Lord; men shall call you the ministers of our God; ye shall eat the riches of the Gentiles, and in their glory shall ye boast yourselves* (Isaiah 61:1-3,6).

This is one of those absolutely fabulous chapters which will be largely fulfilled during the millennial reign.

After casting Israel off for a season, God once again reaches down and restores her to His original purpose—that of giving the world the gospel.

What they did not do as a nation (when Christ came to His own and His own received Him not) they will now do gladly, fulfilling the original intention of God for these chosen ones to be the oracles of His message, the emissaries of His righteousness to the world.

They will be called "the trees of righteousness." What they failed to do originally they will thrill to do for 1000 years!

Jerusalem will be the center of all Christian truth. It will be the spiritual home of the world, where millions will come to worship in annual pilgrimages from the whole world.

> It shall come to pass that every one that is left of all the nations which came against Jerusalem shall go up from year to year to worship the King, the Lord of Hosts, and to keep the feast of tabernacles. . . . In that day shall there be upon the bells of the horses "Holiness unto the Lord"; and the pots in the Lord's house shall be like the bowls before the altar. Yea, every pot in Jerusalem and in Judah shall be "Holiness unto the Lord of Hosts" (Zechariah 14:16,20,21).

The whole world will look upon Jerusalem, Israel, and the Jews as the center of the earth, the center of worship, and the leaders of the world spiritually.

After millenniums of torture, division, bloodshed, and butchery, Israel will be what God wanted her to be and promised she would be—the Promised Land.

The Jews will be God's tools to dispense His message of love to the world. Evangelism will be the theme of the hour for the nation of Israel.

Jerusalem will be a city of peace and the actual home of the Lord.

The bodily presence of the Lord will be seen and heard in Jerusalem at this time (Revelation 20:4).

The sin nature will still be in mankind, resident as the root wanting and capable of bearing the fruit of sin. But with the Tempter bound and out of the way, the earth and the sin nature have rest to a great degree.

The nature of sin in unregenerate man will be inactive as opposed to today's constant activity of evil in all places. The Adamic nature will be present but will be rendered somewhat inoperative by the presence of Christ and His holiness. If temptation is negated and nullified, then sin will be the exception rather than the rule.

The fact that Satan is bound for 1000 years indicates that the propensity for temptation is still resident in unregenerate mankind on earth. When Satan is loosed at the end of this period, all born and alive in human bodies will pass through temptations (as all have in every era of man's existence on earth) in order to be able to use their ability to choose good from evil. This indicates that a sinful propensity is still on earth in the nations.

A large multitude of humans will respond to Satan in his last stand at the end of the millennial reign.

They had to be unregenerated, with their carnal nature leading them into the freewill acceptance of Satan as their evil leader at this time.

9. There will be eating and drinking by the Lord with His saints in the kingdom of God. It will be eating and drinking for worship and pleasure rather than out of necessity.

The humans on earth will be eating and drinking naturally, as before. But there will be little if any drunkenness, since it is not mentioned as happening.

The question has been raised as to whether the saints and immortalized ones will eat and drink with Christ. He said He would eat and drink with us in the coming kingdom. No doubt it will be a spiritual feast, and a memorial to the past blood sacrifice of Christ on the cross. It will be a type of holy communion as we engage in now, except with greater meaning and blessing.

> *Verily I say unto you, I will drink no more of the fruit of the vine until that day that I drink it new in the kingdom of God* (Mark 14:25).

> *Blessed is he that shall eat bread in the kingdom of God* (Luke 14:15).

> *That ye may eat and drink at my table in my kingdom, and sit on thrones judging the twelve tribes of Israel* (Luke 22:30).

10. There will be tremendous differences between today's world and government and that of the millennial government.

Today sin is everywhere in everything. Then sin will be the rare exception.

Today man's governments rule. Then Christ will have complete power throughout the earth. Today Satan controls the minds of men. Then Satan will be bound, and minds will be free from rampant temptation and twisting. Today men are affected by demoniac powers. Then neither demons nor devil will be present.

Today it is the mission of the church on earth to preach the gospel and reach the souls of men. Then there is not word said about a church ministering to the hearts and souls of men.

Today it is primarily a Gentile function to evangelize. Then it will be a Jewish function, as they begin to fulfill the role which God called them to in spreading His Word faithfully.

Today men can escape the law, the courts, justice, and the consequences of sin and evil. Then there is to be a shepherding of the nations with a rod of iron; justice will be swift, pure, and sure.

Today we can only beseech men to accept the claims of Christ as the truth and to do what is right. Then they will be forced to do what is right and to serve the Lord with trembling and fear.

Today is a day of God's mercy and patience with evil. Then there will be a rigid administration promptly executing judgment speedily against anything evil. Today we have a divine toleration of sin. Then there will be no divine toleration of any kind of sin, without speedy retribution.

Today the righteous are to wait and work and have patience for the execution of divine principles on their behalf. Then the righteous will see the work of God on their behalf every day.

Today we are told to wait for our rewards. Then we will have our immediate rewards.

Today many people are embarrassed at times to be called Christians. Then it will be the vogue. Today Christians are harassed, molested, killed, shunned, ridiculed, and considered the offscouring of the earth. Then it will be the sinner who will be the unfortunate one, the one left out, the one to be pitied, the one embarrassed.

Today it is hard to be a Christian, with temptation and ridicule everywhere. Then it will be hard to be a sinner, with righteousness and love and discipline everywhere.

Today nature is groaning, waiting for the adoption by the Lord. Then the regeneration will have begun.

Today the earth is not yielding her abundant increase. Then the abundance of the earth, not torn with nuclear power or ravaged by war, will bring forth greater than our wildest dreams.

Today is a day of death on every hand by many

means. Then will be a day of life and abounding fertility and longevity.

Today a man lives long if he makes it to the age of eighty. Then he will live as long as a tree.

Today the world is torn by political disunity. Then the world will exhibit a beautiful unity of cooperation and brotherhood from sea to sea.

Today is a day of war and bloodshed and man's inhumanity to man. Then there will be a righteous rule, strictly enforced discipline, little death, and virtually no crime.

Today death takes us all. Then perhaps only the unrighteous will die, and that for sins they have committed.

Today sickness and disease rule life. Then healing will be the rule for all.

Today diseases conquer life and limb. Then divine health will conquer disease and prolong life immeasurably.

Today we look and long for the golden age to come. Then the golden age will be here for all to enjoy.

8

God's Glorious Triumph

As though in a final act revealing His infinite, unbounding sense of mercy, judgment, and fairness toward even fallen angels, God looses Satan from his 1000-year prison.

Satan is allowed one last opportunity to tempt those who have lived in paradise and who have been born in paradise.

It seems so unnecessary, so much like the first time, when God allowed Satan in the form of the beautiful serpent to upset His work and creation in the lovely Garden of Eden. Why do it again?

Some divine principle must be served and satisfied, far above our imagination or reasoning, for His thoughts are above our thoughts and His ways are above our ways in everything. Isaiah 55:8,9 explains that truth completely and beautifully.

Satan is allowed to tempt the inhabitants of the earth, and he does so.

Even his incarceration brings no moral or spiritual change in him. His imprisonment makes him even more severe in perpetrating wickedness and evil.

It should be noted that Satan upsets man and man's peaceful ways whenever he can.

Satan is nothing but the greatest of all troublemakers. He never does anything good for mankind. His every act is self-serving and destructive.

Satan goes even to the remote areas of the world to find a following.

Myriads of people will abound again, even after perhaps the greatest majority of the past inhabitants are destroyed by disease, war, the Antichrist, and the justice of God Himself at the coming of Christ.

We entered in this golden age with less than one-third of the population of the world as we know it today.

It is possible that World War Three would have taken 25 percent of the earth's population (Revelation 6:4-8).

It is reasonable to estimate (by the verses of Revelation 9) that another third of the population will have been destroyed at Armageddon. Then came the Lord and destroyed others at the judgment of the living nations.

No statistics are given for those going into the millennial reign, but we can conclude that it will be less than one-third of the original five or so billion that inhabit the world today.

In the last thousand years of world history great changes have taken place in populations, locations, and politics.

America and Canada were born, giving the world North America. Science came into being phenomenally. Oil changed the world. Combustion engines changed power and transportation. Electronics changed communications. And all of this made space travel possible, plus a host of ingenious devices that come during the last thousand years.

In the golden age we will not have wars to kill us, diseases to exterminate us, hunger and famine to liquidate us, and politicians planning against our better way of life.

The free-enterprise system will flourish without the misdirection of the Devil.

The free-enterprise system will flourish on the basis of one monetary system established by the Lord Jesus Christ and His king-priests of this age, who are now immortal.

Dishonesty will be ruled out. Greed will be terminated, and double standards of weights, measurements, laws, etc. will all be done away.

Honesty and integrity will be enforced rigidly in this free-market world.

The law of supply and demand will determine success—not governments buying votes or politicians on the take under the table.

Righteousness will govern business dealings.

I have a feeling that in spite of the fact that Satan is going to be bound and the great tug of man's inner carnal nature will be suppressed to a degree by virtue of Satan being out of the way, the saints will have their hands full administering Christ's new laws for commerce and trade.

But righteousness will always win out. Truth and right will conquer all evil, no matter how innate, subtle, or powerful it may seem at the time.

The rules for business and life have been set for ages. This is the golden age. Nothing and no one can change God's plan for a peaceful, restful earth.

Now the earth is replenishing its populations and rebuilding its peaceful industries for supplies of products to be distributed throughout the earth.

Righteousness and equity that was promised will bring about bathtubs and refrigerators in Africa, not just in America and the industrialized nations. It will be equal rights and privileges for all. Education, civilization, and Christianization will go on throughout the earth in such a marvelous way that everyone will be busy, happy, industrious, and not sorely tempted to do evil. All will share the goodness of the Lord and the land.

There will be no Hitlers, Stalins, or Maos allowed at all. All nations and their government committees will be forced to comply with the righteousness and the proper laws laid down by the Lord Jesus Christ, and His representatives will sit on every committee!

But now, at the end of the golden age, perhaps

even new nations have come. (They did in North America in the last millennium of time.)

Now new governments have formed, and new races have come to replace the old ones lost in Armageddon and the Tribulation judgments.

Civilizations will have moved, changed customs, found new inventions, and discovered new techniques and sciences both of earth and of the heavens.

Those living in the remoter areas of the world will be tempted by Satan and will fall to his whims, even as Satan went to the weaker one in the first temptation in the Garden.

God reveals that man is still a freewill moral agent capable of choosing for himself whom he wants to follow.

God also reveals that mankind will never change, and that there will always be those fools who think that their own way is best.

God reveals that the human mind and soul, when left to itself (even when surrounded by the greatness of God's goodness), is still so ignorant that it doesn't deserve life.

Today the majority of the world's people are against God and His way of life. Followers of the Lord are in the minority.

SWIFT JUDGMENT FALLS UPON THE LOST FOLLOWERS OF SATAN AND UPON SATAN HIMSELF. THE LAST SINNER FALLS.

Given their opportunity to accept good or evil, they take the way of evil. Satan undoubtedly makes great promises to them of "the way it is going to be this time."

He managed to make promises in the beginning, and he still lies to get his plan accepted. Men still listen eagerly rather than go God's way. Human nature is weak.

Fire falls swiftly and punitively upon all, and it is over forever. *This is the last rebellion of man against God.*

It is God's last judgment upon Satan; he is doomed forever; there will never be another chance for him.

Great rejoicing will fill the earth and its redeemed population as they realize that sin is over forever.

The golden age is going to become the golden ages of everlasting eternity. And for those who were faithful, they now receive true, unwavering, everlasting life forever.

THE GREAT WHITE THRONE JUDGMENT OF SINNERS TRANSPIRES, GIVING US THE END OF SATAN, SIN, SINNERS, AND DEATH (Revelation 20:11-15).

It appears in this vision to John that the whole earth and heavens fled away. It is symbolic language indicating the grim seriousness of the situation.

Breathlessly the world awaits the outcome of this judgment of all those who have died unsaved since the beginning of sin with Cain.

Lower hades and sheol empty out their unregenerate souls—those who failed to accept

Christ or God's laws. Now, after thousands of years (for some) of incarceration, they stand before the King of Kings (Revelation 20:11-15).

It appears that in this great tribunal court of the universe, God once again manifests His mercy and His justice by allowing those who are about to be eternally punished the personal opportunity of viewing the existing situation.

Why are they going to miss eternal life? Why are they going to final, unending hell?

Why will they miss heaven and the joys of the universe forever?

Is God fair? Is He just? Is there not some loophole overlooked by them? Is there not some back door to heaven? What about some lesser place or some lesser state of eternal affairs to which they might be sent. . . . some outer planet?

The books are opened containing their unforgiven sins. How easy it is to get our sins forgiven through Christ today! But these rejected and went their own sinful way.

One either follows the flesh instincts or the soul instincts in this life.

Satan always appeals to the strong appetites of the flesh. Christ appeals to the spiritual appetites of the soul and the better judgment of the mind.

Satan appeals to the carnal. God appeals to the spiritual part of man.

Satan offers immediate benefits, though short-lived. God offers a plan that appears to be better down the line than right now.

They accepted Satan's plan for one reason or another. What about you?

No one is missed, for both the land and the sea give up the dead in them.

This is symbolic language, including some symbolisms indicating the omniscience. God misses no one. No one slips by His plan, His program, and His will for mankind.

Unbelief causes a man to miss eternal life with Christ, but his own works of sin determine his degree of punishment.

Faith puts a man in heaven, and his works indicate his rewards.

Lack of faith opens the door to hell. Works of sin determine exactly what happens to the man when he gets there.

All the unsaved are judged according to the works of sin they have done while in this life.

Whoever was not found written in the main book of all, the Book of Life, was cast into Gehenna, or final hell.

Families will be separated forever—children from parents, husband from wife, mother from dad. And the only thing He will ask on that day will *not* be, "Did you join the church? Sing in the choir? Give in the collection plate? Help your neighbors?" No, He will ask, "Did you ever accept my Son, Jesus Christ, as your personal Savior?"

All other arguments fail for qualifying a person for heaven. All other good works or noble deeds fall short of the mark of God.

"Did you ever accept my Son, Jesus Christ, as your personal Lord and Savior?" That will be the question. It is now, as it will be then.

It is not a denominational issue that He is involved with. He will not ask your church affiliation then either.

In this case, it's who you know that counts!

TEMPORARY HELL AND DEATH ARE ENDED FOREVER.

Sheol and hades are now over. They have been the compartments of confinement for thousands of years while God prepared final hell for the Devil and his angels.

Many will follow Satan to his final doom, yet no one is in final hell today, and will not be for another thousand years, until the millennial reign is over.

Death and hell are here somewhat personified, as though they too were created beings that are now being destroyed forever.

Hell being thrown into the fire simply indicates that the temporary place of incarceration is over.

Judgment has done its work, and all who will ever go to hell are now there. The place is forever fixed, and the inhabitants are forever fixed. *Things will never change for it or them.*

The END OF DEATH is a very intriguing statement indeed. Paul said, "The last enemy that shall be destroyed is death" (1 Corinthians 15:26).

Sin, disease, decay, hell, and now death are all part of Satan's realm. It is only suitable that if he is destroyed, he should take with him his works of infamy.

Death is dead! It sounds strange, but that is really what it means.

Death was a very great reality in life with all who were born. Death came to nature—to animals, to birds, to fish of every kind. Death grimly tore life from human beings and devoured life constantly.

But death is now terminated. It was greatly halted during the millennial reign (and little spoken of), but it was not totally exterminated as yet.

But now the crowning act of the victorious Christ has come. He has conquered hell, Satan, sin, sinners, and governments—and now death, the last enemy of God and of mankind, is dead forever!

Death, in a personified form, is cast into hell forever, never to be resurrected or seen again in the world of the living.

Death has taken its last breath of life from man and animal, fish and fowl. It has claimed its last leaf, and now it becomes the personified victim of its own appetite and lust.

What rejoicing there will be with the inhabitants of the earth! What joy in heaven! But what torture in hell!

Whatever hell finally is, it is banishment from all and anything that is good, kind, pleasurable, and tender.

It is banishment from light unto darkness. It is

banishment from all good unto all bad and all evil.

It is unending desire, never fulfilled, never satisfied, but always yearning, seeking, desiring with insatiable lust, without one touch of satisfaction, gratification, and happiness.

Hell could be torture just to be all of these, but it is more. The Lord has not given us a complete picture of what it is, where it is, or all that is involved in it. But enough has been said to let us know that we are glad we are not going there if we have received Christ.

One minute in eternal life will make a lifetime of serving Christ more than worth it all, to say nothing of the joy of living for Christ in this day and age.

To have the Holy Spirit lead us in decisions today is worth it. To have the joy of the Lord as our personal strength makes it worth it. To know our sins are completely forgiven is infinitely worth every effort at being a Christian. And to be given eternal life on top of all of this—it's too much! But I'll take it!

The doctrine of perpetual generations comes to light. Will no one ever die again? Will there be human beings forever? Will there be divine beings? Will there be immortal creatures in incorruptible bodies from this point on?

No, no one will ever die again.

Yes, it appears that there will be human beings forever.

Yes, there will be divine beings, and certainly we will exist forever in our immortal, incorruptible bodies.

Will there be an earth, a city, a heaven? Where will we live?

The earth as we know it will undergo marvelous changes and a metamorphosis never before experienced, but it will not be totally destroyed.

THE EARTH WILL NOT BE DESTROYED.

Too many promises are given in the Bible indicating that the earth will last forever, and that Christ will reign over this kingdom on earth forever, and that God's kingdom will come forever.

We may read verses indicating that the earth will be renovated, but the earth itself will remain.

The words referring to the end of the world really mean a *changing* of the world.

Peter speaks of it as a "dissolving, and the elements shall melt with fervent heat" (2 Peter 3:12). This Greek word for "dissolving" is a word that means "deliverance" or "loosing" more than it does destruction.

The world is to be *loosed*, not destroyed. It is and has been bound since the Garden of Eden calamities. It has been cursed with a curse, but that is about to end, for the curse on nature will be over forever.

That which God intended the world to become and to accomplish has been thwarted until now by His own restraints and judgments upon it. God has held the reins of nature, of nature's development, and of scientific knowledge until now. But now all of God's will, God's plan, God's power is about to break forth and burst the bands as earth is loosed from the injurious, inhibiting forces placed upon her.

Earth is ready to fulfill her task in the original order that God intended.

For six "days" (millenniums) the earth has labored, groaned, and waited. Now her final day is here.

> *We know that the whole creation groaneth and travaileth in pain together until now* (Romans 8:22).

The earth will be cleansed by fire. All the effects of sin, wickedness, godlessness, and the original curse will be lifted at last.

If you have ever seen a flower bloom or a tree grow or nature burst with life, you will know what this means.

Springtime, after a horrible, snowy, cold winter, lets us see a little of what God has in store for His earth.

God never created this earth with its symmetry and beauty and laws of cause-and-effect to be destroyed by the ex-angel from heaven.

It was created to be inhabited forever and never to be destroyed, but always to be in existence, throughout eternity.

> *The kingdoms of this world are become the*

kingdoms of our Lord and of his Christ; and he shall reign for ever and ever (Revelation 11:15).

If Christ is going to have an eternal kingdom in this world, the world has to last forever to fulfill this prophecy.

It would be hard to think, even from an emotional point of view, of this world passing away when you consider what God let happen here that is of value to Him.

Jesus Christ died here, but He also lived among men here. He wept among earthlings, walked and taught among them on this planet, loved them here, suffered for them here, hung on the cross here, and was resurrected here. He sent the Holy Spirit of God to this planet on the Day of Pentecost to lead in the affairs of His church on earth.

He established His church here. It was on earth that the greatest battles between God and Satan were fought and won.

It was on earth that the Jews were chosen to be the deliverers of the oracles of God.

Earthly pilgrimages, earthly sufferings, and earthly victories mark the place where the victories were won and the saints established in the kingdom.

No, no more than God destroyed the earth after He made it and rested on the seventh day will He destroy it now. But He will cleanse it thoroughly from all remnants, impressions, memories, and landmarks of its evil past.

"I saw a new heaven and new earth." Every vestige of iniquity and the curse are gone. This new earth is lovely beyond comparison and defies modern-day language to describe its beauty and wealth.

The heavens have been beautiful in our day. Who among us has not marveled at the beauty of the sun during a sunrise or during a red-hued sunset on a lovely summer evening?

Who has not admired the fleecy clouds of pure white roaming uninhibitedly through the sky?

The soft evening breezes, the warmth of summer, and the thrill of the first bursts of spring thrill us all.

There is something magnetic and majestic about the freshly fallen snow lying on the paths and the mountains, waiting to be walked on softly or skied on daringly down the hill in the grandeur of nature.

Never again will the heavens belch their fire and brimstone. Never again will the heavens allow murderous twisters, hurricanes, or toradoes to tear up lives and rip up the accomplishment of hard-working people.

Plagues, hail, lightning, and thunder will never be seen or heard again in the new world that God has planned.

"And a new earth."

This old earth has delivered her best under the circumstances of the curse. Like a lame man, it has tried to walk. Like a paralyzed man, it has tried to run. Like a bird with a wounded wing, it has tried to fly.

But the cumbersome sin of mankind, coupled with the burden of God's curse, has been too much for the earth.

We can only imagine what the new earth will be like, however, when we see what earth has accomplished in spite of its terrible circumstances and unfortunate weights.

Look at the mountains, the seas, the oceans, and the sand of the seashore, and think of the peace that comes to mind.

Look at the roses, the tulips, the pansies, and the lilies, and think of the loveliness of life that nature gives and shares.

Feel the gentle falling rain, the whisper of the snowflakes as they caress your cheeks, and remember that nature is just bursting to show us her beauty and splendor. Her day is coming soon!

Put your feet in the babbling brook and throw your head back to gaze at the beauty of the birds, the creation of nature around you, and the symmetry and design of such a magnificent earth. Then ask yourself, "What would all this be without the curse?"

Think of nature with her changing glorious seasons to awaken us to the new tomorrows that are ours.

Think of nature's abundance of food and clean water, and its opportunities for science and fun and experiences that are free and yet make up so much of life for us all.

Nature sings, laughs, dances, and leaps around us in spite of the paralysis of the curse and the strangulation of her resources by man's ecological stupidity.

Imagine what it will be when cleansed, loosed, freed, uninhibited, unfettered, and mightily blessed by its Creator, who has been waiting for the time to come to turn nature loose forever.

This new nature will have no black bands to hang on doors or around arms, for there will be no death. No graveyards will pollute city street as grim reminders of yesterday. No death, no suffering, no sorrow will smear her pathway. There will be no devastation, no drowning, no falling, no slipping, no thorns with the roses, no garbage to clean up, no snakes, no carniverous animals, no murderers, no unproductive soil, no plagues, and no sadness because of death or sin.

Imagine an earth where seasons are kind and productive, and no farmer need toil by the sweat of his brow. No woman on this earth has to bring forth a baby with pain, suffering, blood, sweat, and tears.

"And there was no more sea" (Revelation 21:1).

This does not mean that there will be no more sea at all, but no more *danger* in the seas, the oceans. Just as there will be earth and heaven, there will be sea. But the act of regenerating must go to the sea as well as the land and the atmospheric heavens. Many passages of Scripture indicate that there will be seas dividing the land.

The old Rabbis used to teach that the sea will be walked on with as much ease as the earth. Jesus did it, and Peter too (for a short time). It is not unreasonable to assume that the same will be true in this new world.

A NEW CITY CALLED THE NEW JERUSALEM COMES DOWN FROM GOD OUT OF HEAVEN TO ADORN THE EARTH.

This city is the crowning work of God coming to earth. It will light the earth and be the center of the earth's activities, even as the earthly Jerusalem was the center of earth's government and religious activities for the past thousand years of the golden age.

The fact that God brings this city down, and that "the tabernacle of God is with men, and he will dwell with them, and they shall be his people, and God himself shall be with them, and be their God," is the crowning act of all ages.

The Holy Spirit descended in our day during the New Testament era. Christ came as a virgin-born Baby to die on Calvary at the same time.

Christ comes again to the earth to prepare it for its grandest times and to effect His propitiatory work upon mankind.

Now the earth is ready for God. This is the final glory. This is the greatest that could ever be.

God is coming down from heaven to dwell on earth with His creation forever.

God brings His own city which He will share

with the redeemed in their glorified bodies.

All tears, sorrow, sadness, grief, and death is done away with.

God could not appear with these ridiculous human frailties and evils. The world had to be cleansed before God would come to earth to dwell with all those who of their own volition choose to love Him most.

All things now are being made new. God started with man's soul, then went to man's body, then to man's world, and now man will occupy God's eternity and God's unlimited space in the universe.

When the Bible says that God makes all things new, we can only imagine that the brightest of scientific discoveries and accomplishments of our age are in no way to be compared with the scientific discoveries and blessings of the new world, which God will allow us to see, know, understand, and enjoy superlatively.

He that overcometh shall inherit all things (Revelation 21:7).

We are going to inherit things that will take an immortal body and immortal emotions to enjoy, understand, and behold!

We see nothing today as we will see it then. We see no beauty, no discovery, no accomplishment of man or nature that can compare with what is coming then.

> O the depth of the riches both of the wisdom and knowledge of God! How unsearchable are

> *his judgments, and his ways past finding out!*
> (Romans 11:33).

We cannot fully fathom God now, nor will we ever, but we can share His love, His dwelling place, His power, His glory, and His knowledge as He reveals it to us throughout eternity.

Let it never be dreamed that heaven or the coming kingdom of eternity will be boring, inactive, or slow. We will have perfect knowledge of everything and be able to explore the universe without hindrance. Science will be so developed as to make our present day look primitive.

Now we are limited in science, discoveries, computations, achievements, and ambitions, but then there will be no limitations on anything good, beautiful and/or technological.

In describing the glories of this world to come, God also reminds us of who will *not* be there, who will *not* share them in any way, and thus the things we should not be participating in now in any way.

> *But the fearful, and unbelieving, and the abominable, and murderers, and whoremongers, and sorcerers, and idolaters, and all liars shall have their part in the lake which burneth with fire and brimstone, which is the second death* (Revelation 21:8).

One of the tragedies of this text is that the man who is merely fearful or unbelieving is judged and placed with those who are abominable, murderers, and sorcerers (those dealing in false religions, drugs, etc.).

Many people are moral, clean, and upright but unbelieving. Perhaps they had too much education or so-called worldly culture, but they are unbelieving. They do not engage in dastardly deeds as others do, but they all finish life by going to the same dreaded empty place forever.

What is your condition?

Do you know those who are fearful of the reproach of Christianity? Fearful of what others will say about them should they partake of the faith of the believers?

The New Jerusalem is the home of the Lord as well as of the Bride of Christ, the redeemed ones from earth's church age. It suspends the earth forever in glory and perpetuity.

The human race lives on. God's greatest creation, mankind (a little lower than the angels), lives on forever in human form.

This is not to take away from the glorified saints of the church age constituting the Bride of Christ. They are a totally different order of beings now, and will be His ministering servants forever. We will be thrilled beyond all emotions with our position then.

But God's creation will not be destroyed. He made mankind but Satan attempted to ruin them. God has seen fit to destroy Satan, and Satan completely failed in destroying God's plan.

Think of time as being over and eternity as

begun. Time was the era of the probationary laws of God. Time was when you and I lived, and Satan worked his devilish deeds among man.

Time was when wars, sickness, disease, death, and unfaithfulness cursed the earth.

Time is now over in this scene. Mankind and his offspring are no longer on probation. Their eternal, spiritual estate is fixed forever. They are in the same position with God as Adam and Eve were—that of being innocent.

Adam and Eve could sin and were on probation with God. They were tested of the Devil and failed.

This cannot happen again. The "time period" is over. Eternity has begun. We are over with the shame, the degradation, the curse, the period of testing.

All states are fixed forever. The Word says:

> *He that is unjust, let him be unjust still; and he which is filthy, let him be filthy still; and he that is righteous, let him be righteous still; and he that is holy, let him be holy still* (Revelation 22:11).

There will be no more moral or spiritual changes and no more regenerations of man or of earth.

At this stage of eternity, all is as it will be forever. The point is that man is no longer being tested; he is not on probation. He is free, innocent, righteous, and holy; he *wants to live* with God and for God.

There is a city called the New Jerusalem coming

down, and it will be the home of the redeemed in their immortal bodies. But before we touch on that magnificent piece of real estate, let us look at the nations on earth.

Most Christians understand part of what we are talking about up to here. But to tell them that perpetual generations of humans will be on the earth, living in the light of the New Jerusalem forever, is a fact that leaves them speechless. But it is nevertheless true.

Nations will exist forever. Biological reproduction will exist forever. Babies will be born and humans will grow forever. There will be no more death but there will be much life.

Where will they live? What will they do? How will they exist? What kinds of beings will be there?

> *The city had no need of the sun nor of the moon to shine in it, for the glory of God did lighten it, and the Lamb is the light thereof. And the nations of them which are saved shall walk in the light of it; and the kings of the earth bring their glory and honor into it. And the gates of it shall not be shut at all by day, for there shall be no night there. And they shall bring the glory and honor of the nations into it. . . . And he showed me a pure river of water of life, clear as crystal, proceeding out of the throne of God and of the Lamb. In the midst of the street of it, and on either side of the river, was there the tree of*

> *life, which bore twelve manner of fruits, and*
> *yielded its fruit every month; and the leaves*
> *of the tree were for the healing of the nations*
> (Revelation 21:23—22:2).

In these few verses it is revealed that God has a plan for the final perseverance of the human race, though redeemed, purified, and totally fixed in their spiritual estate.

God never intended for Satan to wipe us out. But as in the lesser case of Noah, when most of the populations of the earth perished and God used Noah to replenish the earth, He will do this again finally and permanently.

Noah and his family rebuilt the earth. God will use the remnants from the millennial reign to repopulate the earth.

His earthly crowning creation of mankind will be unusually beautiful, not cursed in any way, and will be able to enjoy the fruit of nature and of the universe forever.

God did not make the planets, the universe, and the heavenlies for just no reason at all.

They have all been placed there with a divine purpose in mind: Man will inhabit the universe. Not now, but then. The books that have been written about man's tenure on earth cannot compare with what we are going to write about millenniums from now. We are going to inhabit eternity and enjoy the program that God has planned so superlatively. It is beyond our imagination and finite comprehension in this body to even begin to understand or absorb it.

It will take a brand new body in a brand new world just to understand the glories he has planned for His own.

This present period of time, known as man's probation period, when man can choose good from evil, will be remembered about as much as we remember Noah and the flood.

Life in the hereafter will be like comparing human form now with animal existence now. There will be no comparison in lifestyle, scientific wonders, marvels of the universe, enjoyments, pleasures, or pursuits of happiness. We cannot, as long as we are in this body, even wildly dream of what life will be like there.

But God in His power and creativity has given us a glimpse of His next new world order.

Outer space will be totally conquered by the nations living then. Mankind will never know a need not satisfied, a thought not expressed, or a desire not explored. All will be for us, and we will be for all.

Interplanetary communication today seems marvelous. Then it will be nothing to have interstellar transportation, complete scientific knowledge, and all the time in eternity to explore the worlds we know nothing about.

God's plan for all the ages to come is for His creation to enjoy the things He has made, has created, and will create forever and ever, without stop, without hindrance, and without an element of fear or sadness.

Fellowship with the Father, the Son, and the Holy Spirit in this great new universe will be the crowning act, the crowning fulfillment of pleasure, the ultimate of all joys for each of us as human beings.

A God who could create this world with its beauty and design, as well as the universe around it with the other planets, will have no difficulty in keeping His own loved ones happy forever. There are no limitations to the mind of God. This means that there are no limitations to what He can do, accomplish, make, and create for us forever.

> *All things are yours: whether Paul, or Apollos, or Cephas, or the world, or life, or death, or things present, or things to come: all are yours, and ye are Christ's, and Christ is God's* (1 Corinthians 3:21-23).

This is a marvelous statement, and even includes things to come that will be ours. Things that are not in existence, things we could never think of or dream of, are all coming abundantly, proficiently, and lavishly. We will enjoy them all without a trace of grief, sadness, weariness, and fatigue. All this for giving ourselves, our sins, and our problems to Him!

If 6000 years of death, sin, sickness, deprivation, wars, tumults, tragedies, natural disasters, etc., has given us almost five billion people and many nations today, think of what one million years will give us!

The nations are going to live forever, with no more of the negatives that have beset us from the beginning. There will be no more falling into sin. There will be no more suffering, curse, and death.

The world to come will make the present world look like it never should have been.

God has had more than one kind of creation before. He has now added to that number of creations.

He has had archangels, angels, and fallen angels. He has cherubs and then He has had humans.

He has added to that list one extra group—the glorified saints, who believed in Him more than anything else.

Their status will be different from those in the nations. Their so-called responsibilities may be different. All that we have to do will be the very soul of pleasure, but we will have obligations to carry out forever.

I do not mean to imply pain, heavy weights, hard word, weariness, and displeasure. It will be an infinite pleasure to serve the Lord.

Whatever our task might be, it will not be a task in the strictest sense of that word. It will be infinitely delightful, marvelously stimulating, and forever grand.

Nations and kings are referred to in these last two chapters of the Bible. God will allow nations in an organized fashion to form. Their government will be of Him and through Him, and all things that exist will exist because of Him and by His power and strength.

He will set kings on earth not in a temporal sense but as His representatives, to bring not so much justice and judgment (for there will be no need of that) but to administer the love, care, and direction that He wants the nations to go in forever.

Science fiction of today will look like nonsense compared with the dignity, the grandeur, the inestimable glories to be revealed to us all in God's great world tomorrow.

THE NEW JERUSALEM WILL BE THE GREATEST REVELATION OF GOD'S GLORY KNOWN TO MANKIND APART FROM SALVATION THROUGH JESUS CHRIST.

Capping the earth, probably with its center over the old city of Jerusalem, will be this city that has come down from God out of heaven.

As early as Abraham, God revealed this city to the human race, and especially to the believers. (Unbelievers wouldn't believe it anyway.)

The city descends. It is from God, out of heaven. Paul speaks in 2 Corinthians 12 about three heavens. One is the atmospheric heaven above us, of which our eyes can see a small part. Telescopes help us more.

The second heaven is the universe of galaxies that we cannot see fully yet, but will see fully when God is ready for us to.

The third heaven is the Paradise of God. This is God's home or dwelling place. Paul saw it.

The city comes down from this third heaven.

It exists now. Christ went to prepare a place for this generation of believers and others to live in it.

> [Abraham] looked for a city which hath foundations, whose maker and builder is God (Hebrews 11:10).

Speaking of the saints of all ages, the Bible goes on to say in this same Hebrews chapter—

> [God] hath prepared for them a city (Hebrews 11:16).

Jesus assured us all and was especially speaking to His earthly disciples when He spoke of this city as a place.

> I go to prepare a place for you. And if I go and prepare a place for you, I will come again and receive you unto myself, that where I am, there ye may be also (John 14:2,3).

Paul referred to this promise by Christ and the revelation given to Abraham when he said:

> Here we have no continuing city, but we seek one to come (Hebrews 13:14).

One of the great texts of the Bible speaks of Christians as coming to this place:

> Ye are come unto. . . the city of the living God, the heavenly Jerusalem (Hebrews 12:22).

It is of celestial origin, and we can only wonder what it will really look like, when we consider the beauty of the earth that its same Maker created many centuries ago.

Its description defies the wildest imaginations to understand and comprehend.

It appears to be suspended above the earth for all to behold as the earth revolves beneath it.

It was not made by earthly hands, and thus its decor and architectural design are significantly different from anything envisioned by mankind.

It is a cube, 1500 miles long on each side.

The glory of God and of Christ lighten it, and it has no need of sun, moon, or artificial light. God's glory permeates every crevice.

The nations on earth use the light of it as they would the sun or moon. They also "bring their glory into it." The city has no need of anything that man could offer it, so the verse must mean that they bring their praise, exultation, and offerings into this glorious place.

Imagine living at this time in a perfect world and realizing that it is perfect because of the sacrifice of Jesus Christ, and having full awareness of what the immeasurable value of His death and resurrection meant to the human family!

Knowledge and understanding of where we might have been or gone will produce such praise, such glory, such eternal gratitude that we will come and they will come to present this glory constantly to God.

The Bible does not say what humans will be doing, but the God who created no two leaves alike, and allows no two snowflakes to be similar, and has had no two fingerprints alike, will not let an hour go by that is not filled with grandeur, glory, happiness, and complete satisfaction.

Because our knowledge will be complete and our emotions fully developed, it will take infinitely more to keep us happy there than here and now. Here we look mostly for happiness and peace of mind, but there we will have so much more to begin with, and yet God in all His infinite wisdom and power will still be keeping every human being superlatively happy forever! That takes an infinite amount of thought, planning, and power. But He has it.

God has built this city out of the prcious stones that we hold so dear on earth—a list of stones so precious that we would never think of them as building materials in the world you and I come from.

The gates are of one huge pearl each. The walls are of jasper, and the city itself of pure, transparent gold. This is something we know nothing of. God uses such purity of precious stones that we know nothing of their value, their purity, or their perfection in this world.

Christ has been preparing a place for you in this city.

The city has 12 foundations and is as high as it is wide and broad. It is 1500 miles up, across, and deep.

The 1500 miles that it reaches in every direction make it greater than one can imagine. It has 12 foundations and 12 gates for each level. Each gate has 12 angels presiding in dignity and glory over that area and entranceway into the center of the city.

The city is as large as the land covering the United States from northern Maine to central Florida and from New York City to Colorado.

In Europe the same city would cover the territory of all of Britain, Scotland, Ireland, France, Spain, Italy, Germany, Austria, and Turkey—and then add half of European Russia on top of that! Imagine how long it would take to explore this city!

This city of gold has streets one-fifth the length of the diameter of the earth. The number of its main streets, boulevards and avenues, if placed a mile apart and mile above one another, would still be over eight million!

That is eight million streets at 1500 miles long each, on which one could walk on transparent gold, lined with mansions, the distance from New York to Denver!

The present earth could not support such a city (as far as available land is concerned) without mammoth changes.

This city will be suspended just above the mountain tops above the earth, with the earth rotating beneath it, receiving its light and love.

The city has a power system unknown to mankind.

The city had no need of the sun nor of the moon to shine in it, for the glory of God did

lighten it, and the Lamb is the light thereof
(Revelation 21:23).

No human failure could count here. No atomic energy is required, nor Arab oil. No nuclear power plants and no coal energy are required at all.

When Moses came down from Mount Sinai, having received the Ten Commandments, his face shone with the glory of the Lord.

When the Shekinah glory of God came down in the temple of old, the priests had to move out because the pressure and brilliance were so immeasurable.

When Paul was caught by the Lord on the Damascus road, he was knocked to the ground by the light, brighter than the noonday sun.

When Jesus was on the Mount of Transfiguration He came down radiating this glory for mankind to see.

God and the Son of Man will be the temple in the city, and thus the entire city will be totally permeated with their presence.

The light of their glory will permeate every corner of every building. There will be no artificial light, for the Word says that Christ is the Light of the world. He always was spiritually and morally, and then He will be physically as well.

No human understanding can comprehend it all. But humans will not need to comprehend it, now or then. For if we could comprehend all that God is, and could totally understand God and His Son and the mystery of the Holy Spirit, then the Godhead would not be God at all. We would be as They are in understanding and wisdom.

We can never understand all of God, nor is it necessary for us to do so in order to enjoy all that He has planned for us.

He has given us in this life all we need to know about Him, His plan, His Son, His Holy Spirit, and the future.

We know all we need to know about salvation and the Lord's coming.

More will be revealed later.

> *The secret things belong unto the Lord our God, but those things which are revealed belong unto us and to our children forever, that we may do all the words of this law* (Deuteronomy 29:29).

> *We know in part and we prophecy in part, but when that which is perfect is come, then that which is in part shall be done away. . .*
> *For now we see through a glass darkly, but then face to face; now I know in part, but then shall I know even as also I am known* (1 Corinthians 13:9,10,12).

Knowledge now is in part. Vision and understanding of God and His ways and plans are partial for us.

But when Christ comes, then all will be known that we need to know to enjoy eternity. Then knowledge will be constantly imparted to us about

God, His universe, and our place in it for all eternity.

There will be no dull moments in God's great tomorrow world. No two days will be alike. No two periods of time will be the same.

The infinite varieties of God will manifest themselves forever and ever.

God's personality, if we may speak of such in human terminology, will never stop producing discoveries and infinite avenues of pursuit for the redeemed humans of His love family.

His Holy Jerusalem will have such illumination, such effulgent glory, that it will lighten the world forever.

The light of His glory will constantly illuminate the souls and minds of the redeemed ones, and will do the same for the nations of the humans on earth, perpetuating God's plan for the universe.

Let the thoughts of tomorrow guide you today. Let the sheer mystique of it all pull you closer to the Lord daily and give you a divine impetus to follow in His steps forever.

Let the love of Christ dwell in you richly, knowing that you haven't seen or enjoyed anything yet compared to the glories and wonders in man's redeemed future.

THE TICKET TO ETERNITY FOR YOU

We often ask about anything valuable, "How much does it cost?"

It is a wise question to ask in this case. There is a

price tag, and it is a costly one for all involved.

The Bible says that "all have sinned and come short of the glory of God" and that "there is none righteous, no, not one."

We are all sinners, one way or another. God knows that.

Jesus Christ was provided as the Lamb of God to be sacrificed for us all, to satisfy the demands of divine justice in payment for our sins.

Christ died and expiated our sins by His blood and death. He rose from the dead, revealing that the demands of divine justice were perfectly satisfied.

"God gave His only begotten Son that whoever believes in Him should not perish but have everlasting life."

Christ came and died, and He did so of His own volition for you and me: "No man taketh my life from me; I lay it down of myself." It was a voluntary death in your place and my place. We deserved it but He took it.

The innocent died for the guilty. God prepared things this way before the foundation of the world for our redemption and salvation. How wonderful His love is!

Now, by recognizing that the prophecies are coming to pass, and by recognizing that you are going to be left out of God's thrilling plan for the ages, and that you are going to be left out of everything except the damnation for failing to believe, *you can believe on Christ and accept His death and resurrection indicating His great love for you.*

By confessing that you are a sinner in need of His grace (salvation, love, and forgiveness), and by simply asking Him for it, God will forgive you, change you, regenerate you, and make you His child for now and all eternity.

Give God your heart in prayer, by asking Christ to come into your life, and by telling the Lord you know you have sinned and are sorry for those sins and believe that He can cleanse you. He will gladly do this.

Faith will fill your heart and soul. You will start a new life, and with new faith you will enjoy living for Jesus Christ every day.

You will read the Bible and pray daily. You will want to fellowship with Christians in church regularly.

You will want to share Jesus Christ with as many people as possible as Christ's witness.

But maybe here would be the best time for me to share my sinner's prayer with you.

I have prayed it with thousands of people in meetings, and on radio and television. By praying this prayer with me you can change your life and your ultimate destiny.

Pray it with me right now, sincerely, in faith believing that God is listening to you just now.

DEAR GOD IN HEAVEN:

I BELIEVE IN YOU. I KNOW YOU ARE REAL

AND I THANK YOU FOR LETTING ME READ THIS BOOK AND FOR HELPING ME UNDERSTAND PROPHECY. I KNOW I HAVE SINNED AGAINST YOU. I AM TRULY SORRY FOR MY SINS. I GIVE YOU MY HEART, I GIVE YOU MY LIFE, I GIVE YOU MY SINS AND MY FUTURE. I NEED JESUS CHRIST AS MY PERSONAL SAVIOR. I KNOW THAT HE DIED FOR MY SINS, AND THAT HE ROSE FROM THE DEAD TRIUMPHANTLY. I ACCEPT JESUS AS MY PERSONAL SAVIOR AND LORD. I ACCEPT YOUR POWER TO KEEP ME. I THANK YOU FOR TOUCHING ME. I THANK YOU FOR BLESSING ME THE WAY YOU HAVE RIGHT NOW. I THANK YOU FOR MY PERSONAL SALVATION. I THANK YOU FOR GIVING ME PEACE, AND I THANK YOU FOR GIVING ME FAITH TO BELIEVE IT ALL.

I AM GOING TO READ THE BIBLE AND PRAY DAILY. I WILL FIND A CHURCH WHERE I CAN GROW IN GRACE AND IN THE KNOWLEDGE OF THE LORD RIGHT AWAY. THANK YOU FOR THE MIRACLE OF MY SALVATION. THANK YOU FOR GIVING ME THE STRENGTH THAT I NEED NOW.

I PRAY THAT I WILL GROW IN THE LORD EVERY DAY AND BE AWARE OF YOUR LOVING PRESENCE WITH ME AS I READ AND PRAY AND WALK WITH YOU.

IN JESUS' NAME I PRAY THIS PRAYER, IN FAITH BELIEVING. AMEN.

You have now entered into the new world of salvation, faith, hope, inspiration, strength of God, and eternal life.

My prayer for you as you read this book and continue to live for Him is that you will grow so steadily and so readily that you will win many others to Him while we still have the opportunity to do so.

If by reading this book you have prayed the sinner's prayer and believe on the Lord Jesus Christ as your personal Savior, write me and let me know about it. I will be glad to send you some free information on growing with Christ and in His grace and knowledge.

Write to: Dr. Doug Clark, at the address on the next page, and ask for the free new-convert material. We want to help you.

DEAR DOUG: PLEASE SEND ME THE FOLLOWING INFORMATION—

- [ ] 1. *DOUG CLARK SURVIVAL LETTER.* Read by thousands on how to survive the coming catastrophes in America and around the world financially. Many have become very secure following Doug's financial advice for the future.

- [ ] 2. *DOUG CLARK'S LIST OF BOOKS ON PROPHECY AND ECONOMICS.* Having written for over 20 years, Dr. Doug Clark has many up-to-the-minute reports to send you regarding world situations fitting into biblical prophecy and your world today.

- [ ] 3. *DOUG CLARK'S LIST OF CASSETTES* on world situations, Bible prophecy, relating current events to your personal situation.

- [ ] 4. Information on buying gold and silver for survival.

- [ ] 5. Information on survival food for emergency purposes.

CHECK ANY OR ALL FOR FREE INFORMATION
Write to: Dr. Doug Clark, P.O. Box 11387,
Ft. Lauderdale, FLA. 33339

RECOMMENDED READING

PROPHECY BOOKS

The Late Great Planet Earth (Hal Lindsey, Zondervan).

The Apocalypse (J. A. Seiss, Zondervan).

The Nations in Prophecy (John Walvoord, Zondervan).

Israel in Prophecy (John Walvoord, Zondervan).

The Greatness of the Kingdom (Alva J. McClain, Moody Press).

They Saw the Second Coming (Doug Clark, Harvest House).

POLITICAL/ECONOMIC BOOKS

The Coming Oil War (Doug Clark, Harvest House).

How to Survive the Money Crash (Doug Clark, Harvest House).

The Control of Oil (John M. Blair, Vintage Press).

The Paper Aristocracy (Howard Katz, Books in Focus).

A Primer on Money (Government Printing Office).